-Minute Chinese Meals

Each Recipe a MEAL, not just a Dish

Madame Yee Yo

Hilit Publishing Co., Ltd.

Publisher: Dixson D.S. Sung
Author: Yee Yo
Editors: Josephine Chou, Brian Klingborg
Designers: Chii-Shuinn Yang, Wen Yu Shen
Photographers: Rick Chang, Ben Lo
Designed, photographed, edited and printed
by Hilit Publishing Co., Ltd.

First Published in 1996
by Hilit Publishing Co., Ltd.
   11F~7, No. 79, Hsin-Tai-Wu Road,
   Section 1, Hsichih Town, Taipei County,
   Taiwan, R.O.C.
   TEL: 886-2-698-4565
   FAX: 886-2-698-4980

ISBN: 957-629-280-8
Printed in Hong Kong

ABOUT THE AUTHOR

The internationally acclaimed author of
You Can Cook Anything Chinese! (1986, 5th
edition 1996; Chinese tanslation 13ed, 1996;
French translation, 1987), Madame Yee Yo,
was born in Nanjing and brought up in
Sichuan by parents who were natives of
Hunan. And she trained under famous chefs
in Taiwan. She has taught Chinese cooking
in the United States for over 30 years.

Now Mme. Yee shows that she is equally
at home with the modern microwave as she
is with the ancient wok! Responding to the
earnest request by the two-professional
family of her son and daughter-in-law, who,
like their peers, have more taste than time,
Madame Yee has developed MEALS that
can be cooked in 30 MINUTES!

She has been the subject of articles in *The
Washington Post*, *Washington Evening Star*,
Washingtonian and the *Potomac Magazine*.
She was Consultant to the U.S. Senate
Dining Room during the 1981 International
Food Festival.

Mme. Yee is married to Dr. George K.
Chacko, Visiting Senior Research Professor
at Universiti Pertanian Malaysia,
Kualalumpur, the 58th country of their joint
travels. Everywhere she studies the local
version of Chinese cooking. They have two
grown children and four grandchildren. She
holds two Master's degrss from Columbia
and Catholic Universities. When they are
not travelling the world, they live in
Bethesda, Maryland.

Dedicated affectionately to
Son and Daughter-in-Law
RAJAH and KAREN CHACKO
Who, with more taste than time,
Urged me to transform timeless Chinese culinary delights
By the magic of ancient woks and modern microwaves
into instant sumptuous treats

Acknowledgments

Favorite guinea-pig *and beloved husband George K. Chacko;* **Faithful**
recipe testers: *Rajah Yee and Karen Elizabeth Chacko, Jessy Bakeman,*
Ronald Hauptman, Gerry Lukenbach, Wanda Maltz, Jo Mitchell, Irene
Schneiderman, Richard Smith; ***Invaluable counsellors:*** *Jerry and Ruth*
Chang, Silvia Chou, Bork K. Lee, Daniel Maltz, Roma Mehta, Gary Roest,
Jia-huei Swei, Yee Qian-hua.

CONTENTS

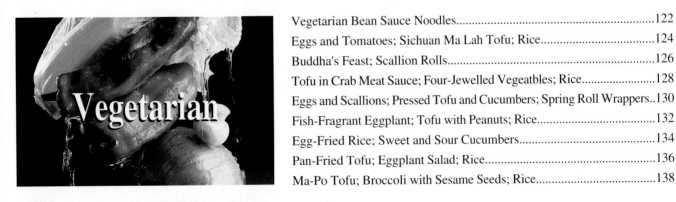

UNIQUE FEATURES OF THIS BOOK

Single Recipe for a Whole Meal: For the first time all dishes in each meal are incorporated into a single recipe. You don't have to spend time making up a meal from various recipes; they are already organized for you.

Make More than One Dish at a Time: The recipes are organized to let you make multiple dishes simultaneously. You prepare as you go along.

Elegant Entertaining: You can use part or whole of these menus to entertain. You can double or triple one menu, or combine two or three menus, except when stir-frying.

Low in Fat: The meals are lower in fat because most often there is only a single stir-fried dish per menu and it uses little oil. The others are either Steamed, Cold-mixed, Stewed, etc. in which very little oil, if any, is added.

Progressive Listing of Ingredients in Cooking Order: The ingredients are listed in the order you use them, with cooking instructions alongside, so that you don't have to waste any time matching them.

Handy Bilingual Shopping List: How should a Chinese name be translated into English? No problem if you take a copy of HANDY BILINGUAL SHOPPING LIST (p. 143) with you.

Individual Shopping List: At the end of each recipe there is a list of PERISHABLES to save grocery listing and shopping time; a list of PANTRY ITEMS to help you to keep the pantry well stocked.

Completely Kitchen-tested: All the recipes have been thoroughly tested by the author, and have been **completed in 12-30 minutes**. Go ahead with complete confidence and Enjoy!

COLOR BACKGROUND DIFFERENTIATION

Main Dish

Accompanying Dish

Rice or Bread

MIX AND MATCH TO CREATE THE MEAL YOU WANT

Choose from any page, for example:

A Main Dish printed on   Beef and Onions on p.54

An accompanying dish printed on   Spicy Cucumber on p.22

A rice or bread printed on   Spring Roll Wrappers on p.46

HOW TO USE THIS BOOK

FAST, FOOL-PROOF WAY TO COOK

To cook delicious Chinese MEALS (not just dishes) in 30 MINUTES.

* Use INGERDIENTS column to organize all the cooking materirals and equipment.
* Use INSTURCTIONS column to proceed step-by-step to cook the meal.
* Ingredients in the INGREDIENTS column have often been bought partially prepared. For example, when purchasing meats, have the butcher slice them for you.
* Save time by doing more than one Step at a time.

EXAMPLE

CHICKEN LO MEIN (Page 28)

Step 1 tells you to put a pot of water on high heat. Don't wait for it to boil, simply proceed to Step 2

Step 2 tells you to marinate the chicken

Step 3 tells you to chop ham and vegetables

Step 4 tells you to boil the noodles. By now you have the water boiling to cook the noodles

SAVE TIME AND TROUBLE

* Read the recipe before shopping for the ingredients.
* Use "Ingredients and Equipment" List to save grocery listing and shopping time.
* Set up the ingredients listed in the left column before you start cooking. Prepare the rest as you proceed.
* Always keep the universal ingredients within reach (they are not listed in Pantry Items): salt, pepper, and sugar.
* Cook two or more things simultaneously by following the steps in the order listed! **BUT,** it is **OK** to move on to the next step if the previous step doesn't require your full attention.
* For dessert, serve fruit (fresh or canned), ice cream, sherbet or frozen yogurt.

ABBREVIATIONS USED IN THIS BOOK

t   teaspoon / teaspoons
T   tablespoon / tablespoons
C   cup / cups
oz   ounce / ounces
g   gram / grams
ml   milliliter

Chicken

CHICKEN AND BROCCOLI WITH HOT BEAN PASTE

TOFU WITH SICHUAN VEGETABLE

RICE

SERVES 4 TO 6

This recipe makes a three-course meal. But if you want to make only one dish, say, Rice, just follow the text printed on

INGREDIENTS	INSTRUCTIONS
• Step 1. Tofu, 1 lb (450 g)	Lift tofu out of water and set on a plate to drain further.
• Step 2. Rice, 11/2 C (360 ml) Water, 2 3/4 C (660 ml)	Wash rice. Place with water in a rangetop casserole. Bring to boil over high heat. Boil uncovered for 1 minute. Turn heat to the lowest setting. Cover and simmer anywhere from 5 to 15 minutes. Keep covered until dinner time. Don't stir. As the rice cooks, do the following:
• Step 3. Chicken, sliced, 3/4 lb (340 g) Soy sauce, 1 T (15 ml) Cornstarch, 1 t (5 ml) Rice wine, 1 t (5 ml)	Mix ingredients listed. Let stand at room temperature.
• Step 4. Broccoli florets, 1/2 lb (230 g)	Cover and microwave on high for 2 minutes, or blanch briefly in boiling water. Plunge into cold water. Drain.
• Step 5. Sichuan vegetable, shredded, 2 T (30 ml) Sugar, 1 t (5 ml) Rice vinegar, 2 t (10 ml) Soy sauce, 1 t (5 ml) Sesame oil, 1 t (5 ml) Scallion, 1	Further drain water from tofu (Step 1). Rinse Sichuan vegetable. Mix it it with sugar, vinegar, soy sauce and sesame oil, pour over tofu. Chop scallion and sprinkle it over tofu. Serve chilled or at room temperature.
• Step 6. Garlic, 3 cloves Ginger, 3 slices Cooking oil, 2 T (30 ml) Hot bean paste, 1 T (15 ml) Soy sauce	Smash garlic with side of cleaver and remove skin. Mince garlic and ginger. Heat wok until very hot. Add oil. Stir in garlic, ginger and hot bean paste. Add chicken (Step 3) and stir until almost cooked. Add broccoli (Step 4), stir until heated. Season with soy sauce and serve.

INGREDIENTS AND EQUIPMENT

PERISHABLES	PANTRY ITEMS		EQUIPMENT

chicken meat, white or dark 3/4 lb (340g)
  (ask butcher to slice thin)
tofu, preferably soft 1 lb (450g)
broccoli florets 1/2 lb (230g)
fresh ginger
scallions
	cornstarch
	rice wine
	cooking oil
	soy sauce
	hot bean paste
	long grain rice
		shredded Sichuan
		  vegetable
		garlic
		rice vinegar
		sesame oil
			wok or large skillet
			microwave oven
			rangetop casserole

MOOSHU CHICKEN

MOOSHU WRAPPERS

"Can I double a recipe?" The answer depends on the recipe. If it is a salad or a stew, doubling is no problem. If it is steamed in the microwave oven, doubling the recipe usually takes one and half the cooking time. But doubling is a definite "no-no" in stir-frying. The secrets of stir-frying are the small quantity and short time. When the recipe is doubled, it doesn't cook fast or well. To serve more people, cook a second dish or another batch of the same dish.

INGREDIENTS	INSTRUCTIONS
• Step 1. Wood ears, 2 T (30 ml) Golden needles, 1/4 C (60 ml)	Soak wood ears and golden needles in warm water. When soft, rinse and drain them.
• Step 2. Chicken, shredded, 1/2 lb (230g) Ginger, 3 slices Cornstarch, 1 t (5 ml) Rice wine, 1 t (5 ml) Hoisin sauce, 1 T (15 ml)	Mix all ingredients listed.
• Step 3. Spinach leaves, 1/4 lb (110 g) Scallions, 3 Eggs, 2 Salt, a dash	Wash spinach. Discard tough stems. Dice scallions. Beat eggs together with salt.
• Step 4. Cooking oil, 3 T (45 ml) Salt, a dash	Heat wok until hot. Add half of oil. Add eggs (Step 3), scramble. Remove eggs when cooked. Pour other half of oil into wok. Stir in golden needles and wood ears (Step 1). Add chicken (Step 2), stir until color changes. Add spinach (Step 3), stir for 30 seconds. Return eggs to wok and stir. Discard ginger. Add salt, garnish with scallions (Step 3).
• Step 5. Mooshu wrappers, 6-8	Wrap wrappers in damp towel. Microwave on high for 20 seconds (or steam briefly).
• Step 6. Hoisin sauce	Place condiment bowls of hoisin sauce on table. Dab hoisin sauce on mooshu wrapper, then add chicken mixture from Step 4, roll up and eat.

INGREDIENTS AND EQUIPMENT

PERISHABLES	PANTRY ITEMS	EQUIPMENT
chicken meat 1/2 lb (230g), (ask butcher to cut into thin strips) spinach leaves 1/4 lb (110g) eggs scallions ginger mooshu warppers	cornstaceh rice wine cooking oil hoisin sauce wood ears golden needles	wok or large skillet microwave oven

RAINBOW CHICKEN
SILVER THREAD ROLLS

"How thick is a slice of ginger?" It is the thickness and size of a quarter, more or less. Don't waste time just to be exact. Don't waste time to peel the ginger either, you are removing the most flavorful part of the spice. Keep the unused portion in the refrigerator as is; or if you use ginger only infrequently, slice it and keep in a jar with a tight lid, covered with wine or sherry. Keep the jar indefinitely in refrigerator.

INGREDIENTS	INSTRUCTIONS
• Step 1. Silver thread rolls, 3-6	Take silver thread rolls out of freezer and wrap in a damp towel. Leave on counter until needed.
• Step 2. Chicken breast, shredded 3/4 lb (340 g) Ginger, 3 slices Salt, 1/2 t (3 ml) Cornstarch, 1 t (5 ml) Rice wine, 1 t (5 ml) Oyster sauce, 1 T (15 ml)	Mix all ingredients listed. Let stand at room temperature.
• Step 3. Cherry tomatoes, 1/2 lb (230 g)	Arrange tomatoes around edge of serving platter.
• Step 4. Green and red bell peppers, sliced, 2 C (480 ml)	Sprinkle with water, cover and microwave on high for 2 minutes. Plunge into cold water. Drain.
• Step 5. Cooking oil, 2 T (30 ml)	Heat wok until hot. Add oil. Add chicken (Step 2) and stir until almost cooked. Add peppers (Step 4), stir briefly. Discard ginger. Arrange on serving platter surrounded by cherry tomatoes.
• Step 6.	Microwave silver thread rolls (Step 1), still wrapped in damp towel, for 1 to 3 minutes. Or steam unwrapped for 5 to 10 minutes.

INGREDIENTS AND EQUIPMENT

PERISHABLES	PANTRY ITEMS	EQUIPMENT
chicken breast meat 3/4 lb (340g), (ask butcher to cut into thin strips) cherry tomato 1/2 lb (230g) bell peppers 1/2 lb (230g), sliced silver thread rolls ginger	cornstarch rice wine oyster sauce cooking oil	wok or large skillet microwave oven

CHICKEN CUSTARD

PEPPERY PEPPERS

RICE

SERVES 3 TO 4

A custard used to take at least an hour to make in a steamer – you had to boil water in the steamer, steam, and wash the steamer and put it away. To make it in a microwave oven is just a cinch!

INGREDIENTS

INSTRUCTIONS

• Step 1. Rice, 1 C (240 ml)
Water, 2 C (480 ml)

Wash rice, place with water in a rangetop casserole. Bring to boil over high heat. Boil uncovered for 1 minute. Turn heat to the lowest setting. Cover and simmer from 5 to 10 minutes. Keep covered until dinner time. Don't stir. As the rice cooks, do the following:

• Step 2. Sesame oil, 1 t (5 ml)
Water chestnuts, 1/2 C (120 ml)
Ground chicken, 3/4 lb (340 g)
Cooking oil, 1 T (15 ml)
Soy sauce, 1 T (15 ml)
White pepper, a dash
Eggs, 3
Water, 2 T (30 ml)
Oyster sauce, 1 T (15 ml)
Cilentro or Chopped scallion

Coat the inside of a shallow microwave-safe bowl with sesame oil. Chop water chestnuts coarsely. Mix with remaining ingredients listed, except for cilantro and oyster sauce. Pour into the oiled bowl, cover and microwave on medium for 6 minutes. Rotate and repeat. Let stand for 2 minutes. When the custard's center is no longer runny, it is ready. Loosen around the edges of the custard with a knife. Cover the bowl with a platter and turn it upside down so that the custard comes out onto the platter. Garnish with oyster sauce and cilantro.

• Step 3. Bell peppers, 3
Red chilies, 3
Fermented black beans,
   1 T (15 ml)
Garlic, 3 cloves
Cooking oil, 1 T (15 ml)
Soy sauce

Meanwhile, cut peppers into thin strips. Slice chili peppers. Rinse away seeds. Rinse black beans. Heat wok until very hot. While wok is heating, remove skin on garlic cloves, chop up garlic. Add oil to wok. Add chilies, black beans and garlic and stir for 10 seconds. Add bell peppers, stir for 2 minutes. Season with soy sauce, serve.

INGREDIENTS AND EQUIPMENT

PERISHABLES	PANTRY ITEMS		EQUIPMENT
ground white chicken meat 3/4 lb (340g)	ground white pepper	cooking oil	wok or large skillet
bell peppers 3 or 1 lb (450g) from the salad bar	fermented black beans	garlic	microwave oven
red chilies	soy sauce		microwave-safe bowl
scallions or cilantro	oyster sauce		
eggs	sesame oil		
	rice		
	canned water chestnuts		

CHICKEN AND RICE STICKS

SERVES 3 TO 4

Unlike wheat noodles, rice sticks don't have to be boiled before stir-frying, therefore, they are simpler to work with.

INGREDIENTS	INSTRUCTIONS
• Step 1. Rice sticks, 1/2 lb (230 g)	Soak rice sticks in warm water while you do the following:
• Step 2. Chicken, sliced, 3/4 lb (340 g) Ginger, 3 slices Cornstarch, 1 t (5 ml) Salt, 1/4 t (1 ml) Rice wine, 1 t (5 ml) Oyster sauce, 2 T (30 ml)	Combine all ingredients listed and let stand at room temperature.
• Step 3. Snow peas, 1/4 lb (110 g) Carrots, 2 whole or 1/4 lb (110 g) pre-cut	Nip ends of snow peas and remove strings. Sprinkle with water, cover and microwave on high for 1 minute. Plunge into cold water. Drain and set aside. Peel and julienne-cut carrots.
• Step 4. Scallions, 2 Cilantro (optional)	Chop up scallions and cilantro.

• Step 5. Mushrooms, pre-sliced in 8 oz
     (230 g) can
Cooking oil, 2 T (30 ml)
Chicken broth, canned,
     1/2 C (120 ml)
Bean sprouts, 1/2 lb (230 g)
Pepper to taste
Soy sauce to taste
	Heat wok until very hot. Meanwhile, drain mushrooms. Add oil to heated wok. Add chicken (Step 2) and stir until almost cooked. Add mushrooms and stir briefly. Add snow peas and carrots (Step 3). Stir briefly. Remove ginger. Pour in chicken broth and bring to a boil. Meanwhile, drain rice sticks (Step 1) and add them to broth. Stir until rice sticks heat up. Add bean sprouts. Stir for 1 minute. Sprinkle on pepper and soy sauce. Garnish with scallions and cilantro (Step 4).

• Step 6. Sesame oil Chili oil Soy sauce Rice vinegar	Use ingredients on left as seasonings. Add as much or as little as you like.

INGREDIENTS AND EQUIPMENT

PERISHABLES	PANTRY ITEMS		EQUIPMENT
chicken breast meat 3/4 lb (340g), (ask butcher to slice thin) snow peas 1/4 lb (110g) carrots 2 or 1/4 lb (110g) from salad bar bean sprouts 1/2 lb (230g) ginger scallion cilantro (optional)	cornstarch sesame oil chili oil soy sauce oyster sauce rice vinegar	rice wine cooking oil canned mushrooms canned chicken broth	wok or large skillet microwave oven

MINCED CHICKEN AND RICE CASSEROLE

DARK AND LIGHT CUCUMBERS

The casserole can be done on a stove, but unless your timing and the amount of heat you apply are just right, you can easily have a burned casserole. To do it in a microwave is far more fool-proof.

INGREDIENTS	INSTRUCTIONS
• Step 1. Rice, 1 C (240 ml) Water, 2 C (480 ml)	Wash rice. Place in microwave-safe casserole dish along with water. Cover and microwave on high for 5 minutes. Rotate, uncover, and microwave on high for 7 minutes.
• Step 2. Ginger, 1 thick slice Chicken, ground, 1 lb (450 g) Salt, 1/2 t (3 ml) Cornstarch, 1 t (5 ml) Sesame oil, 1 t (5 ml) Rice wine, 1 T (15 ml) Oyster sauce, 2 T (30 ml) Cooking oil, 1 T (15 ml), optional	While rice cooks, squeeze juice from ginger with a garlic press onto chicken. Mix chicken with other ingredients.

• Step 3.   Snow peas, 12
Scallions, 2
Water chestnuts, sliced,
   1 cup (240 ml)
Mushrooms, pre-sliced
   in can, 1 cup (240 ml)
	Nip ends of snow peas and remove strings. Chop up white portion of scallions. Chop up water chestnuts. Drain mushrooms.

• Step 4.	Mix chicken (Step 2) with scallions, water chestnuts and mushrooms (Step 3). Spread over top of rice in casserole dish without disturbing rice. Cover dish and microwave on high for 5 minutes. Rotate once at mid-point. Stir in snow peas(Step 3) without disturbing rice. Push raw chicken pieces towards dish rim. Cover and microwave on high until chicken is almost completely cooked, about 2 minutes. Let stand covered for 2 minutes. Uncover and serve.
• Step 5. Cucumber, 1 Soy sauce cucumbers, 2 T Liquid from soy sauce cucumbers, 2 T (30 ml) Sesame oil, 1 t (5 ml)	Peel cucumber, scoop out seeds and slice. Chop up soy sauce cuucumbers. Mix all ingredients listed. Serve cold or at room temperature.

INGREDIENTS AND EQUIPMENT

PERISHABLES	PANTRY ITEMS		EQUIPMENT
ground chicken 1 lb (450g)	cornstarch	canned water chestnuts	microwave oven
snow peas, 12	rice wine	canned mushrooms	casserole
fresh ginger	oyster sauce	rice	
scallion	sesame oil		

CHICKEN WITH SNOW PEAS AND CASHEWS

SPICY CUCUMBER SALAD

RICE

SERVES 2 TO 3

"Can I just cook the rice in the rice cooker?" is a question asked often. Of course, you can. But if you cook in a casserole and serve right in it, you not only save the time for transferring rice into the serving dish, but also have one utensil less to scrub.

INGREDIENTS	INSTRUCTIONS
• Step 1. Chicken meat, sliced, 3/4 lb (340 g) Ginger, 3 slices Salt, 1/2 t (3 ml) Cornstarch, 1 t (5 ml) Soy asuce, 1 T (15 ml) Rice wine, 1 T (15 ml) Oyster sauce, 1 T (15 ml)	Mix all ingredients listed. Let stand at room temperature.
• Step 2. Rice, 3/4 C (180 ml) Water, 11/2 C (360 ml)	Wash rice. Place with water in a rangetop casserole. Bring to boil over high heat. Boil for 1 minute, uncovered. Turn heat to the lowest setting, cover and simmer for 5 to 10 minutes. Leave it covered until dinner time. Don't stir. As it cooks, do the following:
• Step 3. Red chili, 1 Pickling cucumbers, 1 lb (450 g) Salt 1/2 t (3 ml), or to taste Sugar, 1 t (5 ml) Rice Vinegar, 2 t (10 ml) Sesame oil, 1 t (5 ml)	Slice chili open, rinse away seeds. Shred. Slice cucumbers diagonally into oval-shape. Mix all ingredients listed. Serve chilled or at room temperature.
• Step 4. Snow peas, 1/4 lb (110 g) Scallions, 2	Snip ends of snow peas and remove strings. Cover and microwave on high for 1 minute. Plunge into cold water. Drain. Smash scallions with side of cleaver and cut into 1 inch (3 cm) sections.
• Step 5. Cooking oil, 2 T (30 ml) Black mushrooms, 8 oz (230 g) Water chestnuts, sliced 1/4 C (60 ml) Roasted cashews, 1/4 C (60 ml)	Heat wok to very hot. While wok heats, drain mushrooms and water chestnuts. Add oil to wok. Add chicken (Step 1) and stir until almost cooked. Add mushrooms and water chestnuts, stir until heated. Discard ginger. Add snow peas and scallions (Step 4), stir briefly. Transfer to serving platter and garnish with cashews.

INGREDIENTS AND EQUIPMENT

PERISHABLES	PANTRY ITEMS		EQUIPMENT
chicken meat 3/4 lb (340g), (ask butcher to slice thin) cucumbers, pickling 1lb (450g) snow peas 1/4 lb (110g) fresh ginger scallions chili	cornstarch rice vinegar rice wine long grain rice cooking oil oyster sauce	canned black mushrooms sliced water chestnuts soy sauce roasted cashews sesame oil	wok or large skillet microwave oven

CHICKEN IN OYSTER SAUCE

SWEET AND SOUR CARROTS

SCALLION ROLLS

SERVES 3 TO 4

This dinner could be an earth-shaking event! When I cooked it in Taipei, there was an earth-quake (not necessarily because of the cooking). For our picture session, the photograper had meticulously arranged the props, but the earthquake shook the studio on the 8th floor. The bottle tilted, as though slightly tipsy. Saying: "It looks even better slanted!" The photogragher snapped the picture, no doubt to rank with that of the Leaning Tower of Pisa!

INGREDIENTS	INSTRUCTIONS
• Step 1. Scallion rolls, 4	Remove scallion rolls from freezer and wrap in damp kitchen towel.
• Step 2. Frozen green peas, 1 C (240 ml) Wood ears, 2 T (30 ml)	Spread peas on plate to thaw. Soak wood ears in warm water.
• Step 3. Chicken breast, sliced, 1 lb (450 g) Salt, 1/2 t (3 ml) Cornstarch, 1 t (5 ml) Ginger, 3 slices Oyster sauce, 1 T (15 ml) Soy sauce, 1 T (15 ml) Sesame oil, 1 t (5 ml) Cooking oil, 1 T (15 ml), optional	In a shallow, microwave-safe bowl, mix all ingredients listed, then set aside.
• Step 4. Carrots, 2 or 1 lb (450 g) pre-shredded Garlic, 2 cloves	Peel and slice carrots. Smash garlic with side of cleaver to loosen skin. Discard skin and chop garlic.
• Step 5. Water chestnuts, sliced, 1 C (240 ml)	Drain and rinse wood ears (Step 2). Mix chicken (Step 3) with wood ears and water chestnuts. Cover and microwave on high for 4 minutes. Rotate and repeat. Remove cover, discard ginger and add peas (Step 2). Move uncooked chicken pieces to rim of dish. Cover and microwave on high for 3 minutes. Open cover so that the peas won't yellow.
• Step 6. Cooking oil, 2 T (30 ml) Sugar, 2 T (30 ml) Red wine vinegar, 3 T (45 ml)	Meanwhile, heat wok until very hot. While wok is heating, dissolve sugar in vinegar. Pour oil into heated wok. Add garlic (Step 4) and stir for 10 seconds. Add carrots (Step 4), stir for 1 minute. Splash in vinegar and sugar solution. Stir once more. Serve cold or at room temperature.
• Step 7.	Microwave scallion rolls, still wrapped in towel, on high for 1 to 3 minutes. Or steam unwrapped for 10 minutes.

INGREDIENTS AND EQUIPMENT

PERISHABLES	PANTRY ITEMS		EQUIPMENT
chicken breast meat 1 1b (450g) (ask butcher to slice thin)	cornstarch	garlic	wok or large skillet
sliced carrots 1 1b (450g)	cooking oil	water chestnuts	microwave oven
frozen peas	soy sauce	red wine vinegar	food processor
scallion rolls	oyster sauce		
fresh ginger	sesame oil		
	wood ears		

MINCED CHICKEN WITH VEGETABLES

LETTUCE CUPS

STIR-FRIED POTATOES

SERVES 3 TO 4

I served Stir-fried Potatoes at a dinner party. People wondered what the exotic, ivory dish was made of. We played a guessing game. The nearest answer was "a root vegetable" — the guests wouldn't dare to guess that they were eating the lowly potatoes!

INGREDIENTS	INSTRUCTIONS
• Step 1. Potatoes, 1 1/2 lb (680 g) Cooking oil, 2 T (30 ml) Salt, a dash Pepper, a dash	Peel potatoes, then julienne-cut them by hand or in a food processor. Heat wok until hot. Pour in oil, Add potatoes. Stir over medium heat until cooked, about 5 minutes. If you like them crusty, stir them less frequently and cook them longer. Sprinkle on salt and pepper, as much or as little as you like. While stirring, do the following:
• Step 2. Lettuce, 1 head	Use larger leaves, wash, pat dry, and arrange on a serving platter.
• Step 3. Pickled leeks, one 8 oz (230 g) can Water chestnuts, 1 8 oz (230 g) can Carrots, 2 Green pepper, 1/2	Drain leeks and water chestnuts. By hand or with a food processor, chop up all ingredients listed until pea-sized. Then set aside. Make sure the water chestnuts are not over-chopped.
• Step 4. Chicken, 3/4 lb (340 g) Cornstarch, 1 t (5 ml) Soy sauce, 1 T (30 ml) Rice wine, 1 t (5 ml)	By hand or with a food processor, chop chicken into pea-sized pieces and mix with other ingredients listed. Set aside.
• Step 5. Garlic, 3 cloves Ginger, 3 slices Hot bean paste, 1 t (5 ml)	Smash garlic with cleaver. Remove skin and mince with ginger. Combine with hot bean paste.
• Step 6. Cooking oil, 2 T (30 ml) Soy sauce, a dash	Clean wok. Heat until hot. Add oil. Stir in mixture from Step 5. Add chicken (Step 4) and stir until almost cooked. Add vegetables (Step 3) and stir for 1 minute. Sprinkle with soy sauce. To serve: Wrap potatoes or chicken in a leaf of lettuce. Eat with your fingers.

INGREDIENTS AND EQUIPMENT

PERISHABLES	PANTRY ITEMS		EQUIPMENT
chicken meat, either dark or white 3/4 lb (340g) carrots green pepper lettuce fresh ginger	cornstarch soy sauce rice wine cooking oil hot bean paste water chestnuts	pickled leeks boiling potatoes garlic	wok or large skillet food processor

CHICKEN LO MEIN

Fresh Chinese noodles are sold in Chinese grocery stores-refrigerators or freezers. They cook quickly, often done before the water comes to a second boil. You can always tell the doneness by tasting a piece.

INGREDIENTS

INSTRUCTIONS

• **Step 1.**

In covered pot, bring at least 2 quarts (2 liters) water to a boil.

• **Step 2.** Chicken breast, sliced
1/2 lb (230 g)
Black pepper, a dash
Sugar, 1 t (5 ml)
Cornstarch, 1 t (5 ml)
Rice wine, 1 t (5 ml)
Soy sauce, 1 T (15 ml)
Oyster sauce, 1 T (15 ml)

Meanwhile, mix chicken with other ingredients listed. Set aside for later use.

• **Step 3.** Cooked ham, one 6 oz
(170 g) package
Pickling cucumber, 1
Scallions, 2

Cut ham into thin strips. Wash cucumber and cut into thin slices. Dice scallions.

• **Step 4.** Fresh Chinese noodles, 1 lb
(450 g)
Sesame oil, 1 t (5 ml)

Drop noodles into pot of boiling water prepared in Step 1. Cook until *al dente*. Remove noodles from pot and rinse in cold water. Mix in sesame oil.

• **Step 5.** Cooking oil, 2 T (30 ml)
Bean sprouts, 1/4 lb (110 g)

Heat wok until hot. Add cooking oil. Add chicken (Step 2) and stir until almost cooked. Add noodles (Step 4), stir briefly. Add ham (Step 3), stir briefly. Add bean sprouts, stir for 1 minute. Transfer to a serving platter. Garnish with sliced cucumber and diced scallions (Step 3).

• **Step 6.** Soy sauce
Chili oil
Rice vinegar

Use ingredients on left as condiments. Add as much or as little as you like.

INGREDIENTS AND EQUIPMENT

PERISHABLES	PANTRY ITEMS		EQUIPMENT
chicken breast meat 1/2 lb (230g), (ask butcher to slice thin)	cornstarch	sesame oil	wok or large skillet
cooked ham 1, 6-oz (170g) package	rice wine		large pot
pickling cucumber 1	rice vinegar		colander
bean sprouts 1/4 lb (110g)	soy sauce		
fresh Chinese noodles 1 lb (450g)	cooking oil		
scallions	chili oil		
	oyster sauce		

CURRIED TURKEY AND PEPPERS

FIVE-FRAGRANT BABY CARROTS

STEAMED BUNS

SERVES 4 TO 5

Too much leftover turkey from the holiday dinner? Try this easy and exciting menu:

INGREDIENTS	INSTRUCTIONS
• Step 1. Steamed buns*, 8 to 10	Take buns out of freezer and wrap in damp towel. Set aside to thaw.
• Step 2. Baby carrots, 1 1b (340 g) Water, 1/4 C (60 ml) Sesame oil, 1 t (5 ml) Soy sauce, 2 t (10 ml) Sugar, 1 t (5 ml) Star anise, 1 or 2 Scallions, 2 (Don't chop)	Place all ingredients listed in saucepan. Bring to a boil. Cover and simmer until carrots are tender, about 8 minutes (4 if frozen carrots are used). Add a little water if necessary and stir occasionally. Serve hot or at room temperature. Meanwhile, do the following:
• Step 3. Cooked turkey** Bell peppers, 2 Onion, 1	Cut turkey into bite-sized pieces to fill 4 cups (1 liter). Discard pepper seeds and cut into small squares. Chop up onion.
• Step 4. Garlic, 3 cloves Ginger, 3 slices Cooking oil, 2 T (30 ml) Hot bean paste, 1 t (5 ml) Curry powder, 1 T (15 ml) Soy sauce	Smash garlic and remove skin. Mince garlic and ginger. Heat wok and then add oil. Fry garlic, ginger and hot bean paste. Add onion (Step 3) and stir. Add peppers (Step 3) and stir. Add turkey (Step 3) and stir until heated while at the same time adding curry powder. Season with soy sauce. Serve hot.
• Step 5.	Microwave steamed buns, still wrapped in towel, on high for 2 to 4 minutes. Or, steam in a steamer, unwrapped, for 5 to 10 minutes.

* Found in freezer at Chinese grocery stores. If not available, use Brown 'N Serve sourdough dinner rolls.

** Use leftover roasted turkey meat, not the store-bought sandwich meat.

INGREDIENTS AND EQUIPMENT

PERISHABLES	PANTRY ITEMS		EQUIPMENT
cooked turkey meat	cooking oil	garlic	wok or large skillet
baby carrots	soy sauce		small sauce pan
fresh or frozen 1 lb (340g)	sesame oil		microwave oven
bell pepper 2 (3 C from salad bar)	onion, any kind		
steamed buns 1 package	hot bean paste		
ginger	curry powder		
scallions	star anise		

CURRIED CHICKEN

BROCCOLI AND BAMBOO SHOOT SALAD

RICE

SERVES 4 TO 6

If you use 2 cups of water for 1 cup of rice, why use 2 3/4 cups of water for 1 1/2 cups of rice? It's not Chinese arithmetic, but a gourmet secret: decrease the proportion of the water as you increase the quantity.

INGREDIENTS	INSTRUCTIONS
• Step 1. Small fryer, 1, chopped together with bones Salt, 1 t (5 ml) Curry powder, 1 1/2 T (22 ml) Black pepper, 1/2 t (3 ml) Rice wine, 1 t (5 ml) Soy sauce, 1 T (15 ml)	Mix ingredients listed.
• Step 2. Rice, 1 1/2 C (360 ml) Water, 2 3/4 C (660 ml)	Wash rice. Place with water in a rangetop casserole. Bring to boil over high heat. Boil for 1 minute uncovered. Turn heat to the lowest setting, cover and simmer for 5 to 10 minutes. Keep covered until dinner time. Don't stir. While the rice cooks, do the following:
• Step 3. Small onion, 1 Potatoes, 2	Chop up onion. Cut potatoes into chunks (peeling optional).
• Step 4. Cooking oil, 2 T (30 ml) Water, 1 1/4 C (300 ml)	Heat wok until very hot. Pour in oil. Add onion (Step 3) and stir briefly. Add chicken (Step 1) and stir until color changes. Add potatoes (Step 3) and stir 1 minute. Add water, bring to a boil. Turn heat to medium, cover and simmer for 8 to 10 minutes, stirring occasionally. Serve with rice.
• Step 5. Broccoli florets, 3/4 lb (340 g) Bamboo, sliced, one 8 oz (230 g) can Salt, 3/4 t (4 ml) Sugar, 1 T (15 ml) Sesame oil, 2 t (10 ml) Rice vinegar, 1 T (15 ml)	Sprinkle 1 T (15 ml) water on broccoli, cover and microwave on high for 2 minutes. Plunge into cold water. Drain. Combine with rest of ingredients listed, mix well, serve chilled or at room temperature.

INGREDIENTS AND EQUIPMENT

PERISHABLES	PANTRY ITEMS		EQUIPMENT

fryer 1 small
  (ask butcher to cut into bite-size picese,
  skinning optional)
broccoli florets 3/4 lb (340g)
	cornstarch
	rice wine
	rice vinegar
	cooking oil
	sesame oil
	curry powder
		soy sauce
		onions, any kind
		boiling potatoes
		canned and sliced
		  bamboo shoots
		long grain rice
			wok or large skillet
			  with cover
			microwave oven
			medium rangetop
			  casserole

CHICKEN STEWED IN BLACK BEAN SAUCE

SNOW PEAS, BABY CORN AND WATER CHESTNUTS

RICE

SERVES 5 TO 6

This chicken dish is great for any pot luck dinner. Not just the pot, but you, too, are lucky—because you will get a lot of "ooo"s and "aah"s, and will be hailed as the best cook in town. Just don't tell anyone how easy it is (That's a violation of Gourmet Cooks Trade Secrets Act!).

	INGREDIENTS	INSTRUCTIONS
• Step 1.	Small fryer, 1, Chopped together with bones Salt, 1 t (5 ml) Cornstarch, 2 t (10 ml) Rice wine, 1 T (15 ml)	Mix ingredients listed.
• Step 2.	Rice, 1 1/2 C (360 ml) Water, 2 3/4 C (660 ml)	Wash rice. Place with water in a rangetop casserole. Bring to boil over high heat. Boil uncovered for 1 minute. Turn heat to the lowest setting, cover and simmer anywhere between 5 to 10 minutes. Let stay coverd until dinner is served. Don't stir.
• Step 3.	Garlic, 5 cloves Fermented black beans, 2T (30 ml) Ginger, 5 slices	Smash garlic and remove skin. Mince along with additional ingredients listed.
• Step 4.	Cooking oil, 2 T (30 ml) Sugar, 1 T (30 ml) Soy sauce, 3 T (45 ml) Water, 1 C (240 ml) Cornstarch, 1 T (15 ml) Water, 1 T (15 ml) Seallion, 1	Heat wok until very hot. Add oil. Add ingredients from Step 3 and stir briefly. Add chicken (Step 1), and stir until color changes, while adding sugar and soy sauce. Splash in water. Transfer to rangetop casserole dish. Bring to boil, then turn heat to simmer. Cook until chicken is done, about 8 to 10 minutes. Mix cornstarch with water to make a paste. Add it to chicken to thicken the sauce. Chop scallion and garnish.
• Step 5.	Snow peas, 1/4 lb (110 g) Baby corn, one 16 oz (450 g) can Water chestnuts, slices, 1 small can Cooking oil, 2 T (30 ml) Chicken bouillon powder, 1 T (15 ml) Black pepper, 1/4 t (1 ml) Rice wine, 1 T (15 ml)	Nip ends of snow peas and remove strings. Wash wok, then heat until very hot. Drain baby corn and chestnuts. Add oil to wok. Add vegetables separately in order listed, stirring briefly each time. Sprinkle in bouillon and pepper. Splash in wine. Stir once more, then serve.

INGREDIENTS AND EQUIPMENT

PERISHABLES	PANTRY ITEMS		EQUIPMENT
fryer 1 (ask butcher to chop into bite-size pieces, skinning optional) snow peas 1/4 1b (110g) fresh ginger scallion	cornstarch chicken bouillon powder long grain rice fermented black beans rice wine canned baby corn	canned wtaer chestnuts cooking oil soy sauce garlic	wok or large skillet 2 rangetop casseroles

CHICKEN CUTLETS WITH ALMONDS

RAINBOW PEPPERS

SILVER THREAD ROLLS

SERVES 4

No chopsticks for a Chinese dinner? You bet! This kind of dining is what the Chinese call "a Chinese dinner served in the Western style".

INGREDIENTS	INSTRUCTIONS
• Step 1. Silver thread rolls*, 4-6	Remove from freezer and wrap in damp towel.
• Step 2. Ginger, 1 thick slice Salt, 3/4 t (4 ml) Cornstarch, 1 t (5 ml) Rice wine, 1 t (5 ml) Chicken breast, boneless and halved, 2 pairs	Squeeze juice from ginger using a garlic press. Mix with salt, cornstarch and wine. Rub mixture over chicken, set aside.
• Step 3. Small onion, 1 Bell peppers, red, green, yellow, 1 each	Peel and halve onion, cut into strips. Halve peppers, wash away seeds, discard stems, cut into strips.
• Step 4. Cooking oil, 1 T (15 ml) Oyster sauce, 1 T (15 ml) Ketchup, 2 T (30 ml) Water, 1/3 C (80 ml) Roasted almonds, 2 T (30 ml)	Heat skillet over medium heat. Add oil. Brown chicken pieces (Step 2) on both sides. Add oyster sauce, ketchup and water. Cover and simmer, turning chicken occasionally, until chicken is cooked and only a thin layer of liquid remains. Transfer onto serving platter and garnish with almonds. Serve hot.
• Step 5. Cooking oil, 1 T (15 ml) Rice wine, 1 T (15 ml) Salt, a dash Pepper, a dash	As the chicken cooks, heat wok over high heat. Swirl in oil. Add onion (Step 3) and stir for 1 minute. Add bell peppers (Step 3) and stir for 1 minute. Add the remaining ingredients. Stir once more and serve.
• Step 6.	Microwave silver thread rolls, still wrapped in damp towel, for 1 to 3 minutes (or steam, unwrapped for 5 to 15 minutes.)

* Substitute with Brown N' Serve dinner rolls. Wrap in damp towel and microwave until hot, about 1 minute.

INGREDIENTS AND EQUIPMENT

PERISHABLES	PANTRY ITEMS		EQUIPMENT
chicken breast 2 pairs, boned, skinned and split	cornstarch	roasted almonds	skillet with cover
peppers of various colors	oyster sauce	onion, any kind	wok
silver thread rolls	rice wine		microwave oven
fresh ginger	cooking oil		
	ketchup		

CHICKEN AND VEGETABLE CHOWDER

HAM AND PEPPERS

SPRING ROLL WRAPPERS

SERVES 3 TO 4

The chowder and a starch make a meal; so do Ham and Peppers with a starch. Of course, you can mix and match from menus.

	INGREDIENTS	INSTRUCTIONS
• Step 1.	Green peppers, 2 Ham, sliced, one 6 oz (170 g) package	Halve peppers. Wash away seeds and discard stems. Cut into strips. Cut across the stack of ham to make strips also.
• Step 2.	Chicken broth, two 14 oz (400 g) cans Water, 1 C (240 ml)	Bring broth and water to a boil in rangetop casserole dish or pot.
• Step 3.	Ground Chicken, 1/4 lb (110 g) Salt, 1/4 t (1 ml) Rice wine, 1 t (5 ml) Egg whites, 3	Mix chicken with salt and wine. Then stir in egg white.
• Step 4.	Tomato, 1 Water chestnuts, 1/2 C (120 ml) Frozen green peas, 1/2 C (120 ml) Cornstarch, 2 T (30 ml) Water, 2 T (30 ml) White pepper, a dash	Dice tomato and water chestnuts. Add tomato to boiling water and broth mixture (Step 2). Wait until mixture returns to a boil, then add water chestnuts. When mixture returns to a boil again, add peas. Mix cornstarch and water to make a paste. Stir paste into mixture to thicken. Add chicken (Step 3), stirring constantly. Then turn off heat, sprinkle pepper on top and keep warm until ready to serve.
• Step 5.	Scallion, 1 Cooking oil, 1 T (15 ml) Fermented black beans, 1 T (15 ml) Soy sauce, 1 t (5 ml)	Heat wok until very hot. As the wok heats, chop scallion and set aside. Add oil to wok. Add black beans and stir briefly. Add peppers (Step 1), stir for 2 minutes. Add ham (Step 1) and stir until heated. Stir in soy sauce and scallion.
• Step 6.	Spring roll wrappers, 15-20	Wrap wrappers in damp towel. Microwave on high for 20 to 40 seconds (or steam briefly). Wrap ham and green peppers in spring roll wrappers to eat.

INGREDIENTS AND EQUIPMENT

PERISHABLES	PANTRY ITEMS	EQUIPMENT
ground chicken; 1/4 lb (110g)	white pepper	wok or large skillet
sliced ham, one 6 oz (170g) package	soy sauce	small rangetop cassserole
tomato 1	cooking oil	
frozen green peas	rice wine	
spring roll wrappers	cornstarch	
eggs	canned water chestnuts	
scallions	canned chicken broth	
green peppers 2	fermented black beans	

Beef

TANGERINE BEEF BALLS

BROCCOLI AND BABY CORN SALAD

RICE

SERVES 3 TO 4

Dried tangerine peel from the Chinese grocery stores gives the beef balls the distinct flavor. Orange peel from the supermarket is not a good substitute. The former takes about 15 minutes to soften. If you can't finish this menu in 30 minutes, don't blame me. Blame the tangerine peel!

INGREDIENTS	INSTRUCTIONS
• Step 1. Dried tangerine peels, 2	Soak peels in hot water.
• Step 2. Rice, 1 C (240 ml) Water, 2 C (480 ml)	Wash rice. Place with water in a rangetop casserole. Bring to boil over high heat. Boil for 1 minute, uncovered. Turn heat to the lowest setting, cover and simmer for 5 to 10 minutes. Keep covered until dinner time. Don't stir. While the rice cooks, do the following:
• Step 3. Broccoli florets, 1/2 lb (230 g) Baby corn, one 8 oz (230 g) can Sugar, 1 t (5 ml) Rice vinegar, 1 t (5 ml) Sesame oil, 1 t (5 ml) Soy sauce, 1 t (5 ml) Chili oil, 1 t (5 ml), optional Salt, a dash	Sprinkle broccoli with a little water, cover and microwave on high for 1 minute. Plunge into cold water. Drain. Drain baby corn. Mix all ingredients listed. Serve cold or at room temperature.
• Step 4. Watercress, 1 bunch	Wash watercress and use it to line a shallow microwave-safe bowl.
• Step 5. Scallions, 2 Cilantro, 1 sprig Water chestnuts, 1 C (240 ml) Ground chuck, 1 lb (450 g) Ground pepper, 1/4 t (1 ml) Sugar, 1 t (5 ml) Cornstarch, 1 T (15 ml) Sesame oil, 1 t (5 ml) Cooking oil, 1 T (15 ml), optional Rice wine, 1 T (15 ml) Oyster sauce, 1 T (15 ml) Soy sauce, 1 T (15 ml) Egg white, 1	Chop white portion of scallions, cilantro and water chestnuts. Mix all ingredients listed.
• Step 6.	Drain tangerine peels when softened. Mince fine. Combine with meat mixture (Step 5). Shape into 12 meatballs. Add flour if necessary. Set meatballs on watercress. Cover and microwave on high for 3 minutes. Rotate, then microwave for an additional 3 minutes. Let stand for 2 minutes, then remove cover. Serve.

INGREDIENTS AND EQUIPMENT

PERISHABLES	PANTRY ITEMS		EQIUPMENT
ground chuck 1 lb (450g)	cornstarch	oyster sauce	microwave oven
broccoli florets 1/2 lb (230g)	sesame oil	rice	small rangetop casserole
watercress 1 bunch	rice wine	canned water chestnuts	shallow microwaveable bowl
scallions	rice vinegar	canned baby corn	
cilantro	cooking oil	dried tangerine peel	
eggs	soy sauce	chili oil	

SICHUAN BEEF CUSTARD

CURRIED GREEN BEANS

RICE

SERVES 3 TO 4

The beef dish is spicy, but the green bean dish is even spicier. If you simply love spices, try this easy menu.

INGREDIENTS

INSTRUCTIONS

• Step 1.
Rice, 1 C (240 ml)
Water, 2 C (480 ml)

Wash rice. Place with water in a rangetop casserole. Bring to boil over high heat. Boil uncovered for 1 minute. Turn heat to the lowest setting, cover and simmer anywhere between 5 to 10 minutes. Let stay covered until dinner is served. Don't stir.

• Step 2.
Water chestnuts, 1/2 C (120 ml)
Sichuan vegetable, shredded,
   1/2 C (120 ml)
Beef, ground, 3/4 lb (340 g)
Soy sauce, 1 T (15 ml)
Cooking oil, 1 T (15 ml), optional
Eggs, 3
Cilantro or chopped scallions

Chop up water chestnuts. Rinse Sichuan vegetable. Mix all ingredients listed, except cilantro. Pour into shallow, microwave-safe bowl. Cover and microwave on medium for 6 minutes. Rotate and repeat. Let stand for 2 minutes. Garnish with cilantro.

• Step 3.
Garlic, 3 cloves
Cooking oil, 1 T (15 ml)
Frozen green beans,
   16 oz (450 g)
Curry powder, 1 T (15 ml)
Black pepper, 1/2 t (3 ml)
Water, 1/4 C (60 ml)
Soy sauce

Meanwhile, heat wok until very hot. Smash garlic ① to loosen skin. Discard skin and mince garlic. Add oil to wok. Add garlic and stir. Add green beans and stir. Break up icy chunks ② if necessary. Add curry powder and pepper. When green beans are fully heated, add water, cover and steam for 2 minutes. Uncover and continue to stir over high heat until cooked, about 5 minutes. Add soy sauce to taste and serve.

①

②

INGREDIENTS AND EQUIPMENT

PERISHABLES	PANTRY ITEMS	EQUIPMENT
ground beef 3/4 lb (340g)	black pepper	wok or large skillet
frozen green beans 16oz (450g)	cooking oil	small rangetop casserole
eggs	soy sauce	microwave oven
cilantro or scallions	rice	
	water chestnuts	
	shredded Sichuan vegetable	
	curry powder	
	garlic	

CURRIED MINCED BEEF WITH VEGETABLES
SPRING ROLL WRAPPERS

SERVES 2 TO 3

"What, it took you only 15 minutes to cook this beautiful meal?" "Shhh! Gourmet Cooks Trade Secrets Act!"

INGREDIENTS

- Step 1. Beef, ground, 3/4 lb (340 g)
  Cornstarch, 1 t (5 ml)
  Rice wine, 1 t (5 ml)
  Soy sauce, 1 T (15 ml)

- Step 2. Garlic. 3 cloves
  Onion, 1
  Potato, 1

- Step 3. Cooking oil, 2 T (30 ml)
  Curry powder, 1 T (5 ml)
  Soy sauce, 1 T (15 ml)
  Black pepper, 1/2 t (3 ml)*
  Mixed frozen vegetables,
    10 oz (280 g)

- Step 4. Water, 1/4 C (60 ml)
  Soy sauce

- Step 5. Spring roll wrappers, 10-15

INSTRUCTIONS

Mix all ingredients listed and let stand at room temperature.

Smash garlic and remove skin. Mince garlic. Dice onion and potato.

Heat wok until very hot. Add oil. Add garlic (Step 2) and stir briefly. Add onion (Step 2) and stir until fragrant. Add beef (Step 1), stir until it is almost cooked while at the same time adding curry powder, soy sauce and pepper. Next, add potato (Step 2) and stir for 1 minute. Add mixed frozen vegetables and stir. Break up icy chunks if necessary.

When mixed frozen vegetables have heated up, add water, cover and steam for 2 minutes. Uncover and stir occasionally while continuing to cook over high heat until vegetables are tender, about 5 minutes. Sprinkle with soy sauce to taste and serve along with spring roll wrappers.

Wrap wrappers in damp towel and microwave on high for 15 to 30 seconds, or steam briefly. Roll up beef and vegetable dish in wrappers to eat.

* The dish is biting hot as it should be. If you prefer a milder taste, use less pepper.

INGREDIENTS AND EQUIPMENT

PERISHABLES	PANTRY ITEMS		EQUIPMENT
ground beef 3/4 lb (340g)	black pepper	cooking oil	microwave oven
spring roll wrappers	cornstarch	curry powder	wok or large skillet
frozen mixed vegetables 10oz (280g)	rice wine	onions, any kind	
	soy sauce	boiling potatoes	
		garlic	

ANTS ON TREE

BROCCOLI AND CARROT SALAD

STEAMED BUNS

SERVES 2 TO 3

Don't worry, you don't have to catch any ant or chop down a tree! To the creator of this dish, the dark ground meat must have looked like ants and the bean threads as the branches of a tree. The bean thread can be either fried or stir-fried. To make it in 30 minutes, you have no choice but to stir-fry. Even though the threads look like noodles, Chinese use them as a protein rather than as starch food. They are made of mung beans.

INGREDIENTS	INSTRUCTIONS
• Step 1. Steamed buns, 4-6	Wrap buns in damp towel. Set aside.
• Step 2. Bean threads, 4 oz (110 g) Beef, ground, 1/2 lb (230 g) Red pepper, crushed, 1/4 t (1 ml) or to taste Cornstarch, 1 t (5 ml) Rice wine, 1 t (5 ml) Dark soy sauce, 1 T (15 ml) Oyster sauce, 1 T (15 ml)	Soak bean threads in warm water until ready to use. Mix beef with remaining ingredients listed.
• Step 3. Broccoli florets, 1/2 lb (230 g) Salt, 1/2 t (3 ml) Sugar, 1 t (5 ml) Rice vinegar, 1 T (15 ml) Sesame oil, 1 t (5 ml) Chili oil, 1 t (5 ml) Carrots, 2, or 1/4 lb (110 g) ready-shredded	Cover broccoli and microwave on high for 1 1/2 minutes. Plunge into cold water. Drain and mix with all remaining ingredients, except for carrots. Next, shred carrots by hand or in food processor. Remove broccoli from liquid. Arrange broccoli on a serving platter. Reserve liquid. Scatter carrots on top of broccoli. Pour liquid over top of both. Serve chilled or at room temperature.
• Step 4.	Microwave buns still wrapped in towel on high for 1 to 3 minutes, or steam for 5 to 15 minutes.
• Step 5. Cooking oil, 2 T (30 ml) Scallion, 1 Beef broth, canned, 1 C (240 ml)	Heat wok until very hot. While wok heats up, dice scallion. Add oil to wok. Add beef mixture (Step 2) and stir until almost cooked. Add broth. When broth comes to a boil, take bean threads out of water (Step 2) and combine with beef in wok, stirring constantly for 1 minute. Sprinkle scallion on top and serve.

INGREDIENTS AND EQUIPMENT

PERISHABLES	PANTRY ITEMS		EQUIPMENT
ground beef 1/2 lb (230g)	cornstarch	oyster sauce	wok or large skillet
broccoli florets 1/2 lb (230g)	rice wine	sesame oil	microwave oven
carrots	rice vinegar	bean threads	
scallions	cooking oil	crushed red pepper	
steamed buns	chili oil	canned beef broth	
	dark soy sauce		

BEEF AND ASPARAGUS IN HOISIN SAUCE

CAULIFLOWER WITH DRIED SHRIMP

MOOSHU WRAPPERS

SERVES 2 TO 3

"Phew! What an awful smell!" Students often hold their noses when I introduce dried shrimp to them. However, once it is put in a dish, many change their mind. Hold off your verdict at the first whiff, give the poor shrimp the benefit of the doubt— it's the American way!

INGREDIENTS	INSTRUCTIONS
• Step 1. Dried shrimp, 3 T (45 ml) Warm water, 3 T (45 ml)	Soak dried shrimp in warm water.
• Step 2. Flank steak, sliced 3/4 lb (340 g) Ginger, 3 slices Cornstarch, 1 t (5 ml) Rice wine, 1 t (5 ml) Hoisin sauce, 1 T (15 ml) Soy sauce, 1 T (15 ml)	Mix all ingredients listed. Let stand at room temperature until ready to cook.
• Step 3. Asparagus, 1 lb (450 g)	Remove tough bottom ends of asparagus. Cut asparagus diagonally into thin slices.
• Step 4. Cauliflower florets, 3/4 lb (340 g)	Cut into bite-sized pieces.
• Step 5. Cooking oil, 2 T (30 ml) Salt Pepper	Heat wok until very hot. Drain water from shrimp (Step 1), but reserve water. Add oil to wok, add shrimp and stir for 10 seconds. Add cauliflower (Step 4) and stir for 1 minute. Splash in water used for soaking shrimp. Stir until cauliflower is tender. Season with salt and pepper and serve.
• Step 6. Cooking oil, 2 T (30 ml)	Rinse wok and heat until hot again. Add oil. Add flank steak (Step 2) and stir until almost cooked. Add asparagus (Step 3). Stir for 1 minute. Discard ginger and serve. Don't overcook.
• Step 7. Mooshu wrappers, 6-8 Hoisin sauce	Wrap wrappers in damp towel and microwave on high heat for 20 to 40 seconds, or steam briefly. Put condiment bowls of hoisin sauce on the table. Spread hoisin sauce on a wrapper, add steak, roll up and eat, using your fingers. Eat the cauliflower and shrimp in the same manner or use chopsticks.

INGREDIENTS AND EQUIPMENT

PERISHABLES	PANTRY ITEMS	EQUIPMENT
flank steak 3/4 lb (340g) (ask butcher to slice thin) asparagus 1 lb (450g) cauliflower florets 3/4 lb (340g) ginger mooshu wrappers	cornstarch rice wine hoisin sauce soy sauce cooking oil dried shrimp	wok or large skillet microwave oven

BEEF AND RICE CASSEROLE

CELERY WITH SOY SAUCE CUCUMBERS

Soy sauced cucumbers are baby cucumbers cut into strips and preserved in soy sauce, packed in cans or jars, often misleadingly labelled as "pickled cucumbers".

INGREDIENTS	INSTRUCTIONS
• Step 1. Rice, 1 C (240 ml) Water, 2 1/4 C (540 ml)	Wash rice. Place along with water in microwave-safe casserole dish. Cover and microwave on high for 5 minutes. Rotate, uncover, and microwave on high until most moisture is gone, about 7 minutes. Meanwhile, do the following:
• Step 2. Beef, ground, 1 lb (450 g) Cornstarch, 2 t (10 ml) Rice wine, 1 T (15 ml) Oyster sauce, 2 T (30 ml) Cooking oil, 1 T (15 ml), optional	Mix all ingredients listed. Set aside.
• Step 3. Celery, 5 stalks, or 3/4 lb (340 g) from salad bar Sugar, 1 t (5 ml) Soy sauce cucumbers, 1/4 C (60 ml) Liquid from cucumbers, 1 T (15 ml) Sesame oil, 1 t (5 ml)	Wash celery. Slice thinly. Mince soy sauce cucumbers. Mix all ingredients listed. Serve chilled or at room temperature.
• Step 4. Onion, 1 Water chestnuts, 1 C (240 ml)	Chop up onions and water chestnuts. Mix with beef mixture prepared in Step 2. When the rice (Step 1) is ready, spread over top of rice directly in the casserole dish. Cover and microwave on high for 2 minutes. Stir meat and vegetable mixture without disturbing the rice. Push undercooked meat to edges of dish. Cover and microwave on high for 2 more minutes.
• Step 5. Cilantro or parsley	Garnish casserole with cilantro or parsley and serve.

INGREDIENTS AND EQUIPMENT

PERISHABLES	PANTRY ITEMS		EQUIPMENT
ground sirloin or chuck 1 lb (450g) celery cilantro	cornstarch long grain rice soy sauce cooking oil sesame oil	oyster sauce rice wine soy sauce cucumbers canned water chestnuts onions, any kind	microwaveable casserole microwave oven

BEEF AND ONIONS

SPICY CUCUMBERS

RICE

SERVES 2 TO 3

To save time, ask the butcher to slice beef thin; and grab cut-up onions from the salad bar. To cook only the beef dish it takes less than 10 minutes. Just follow the text printed on _____ . *What are you going to do with all that spare time?*

INGREDIENTS	INSTRUCTIONS
• Step 1. Rice, 3/4 C (180 ml) Water, 1 1/2 C (360 ml)	Wash rice. Place with water in a rangetop casserole. Bring to boil over high heat. Boil for 1 minute, uncovered. Turn heat to the lowest setting, cover and simmer for 5 to 10 minutes. Leave it covered until dinner time. Don't stir. As it cooks, do the following:
• Step 2. Flank steak, thinly sliced, 1 lb (450 g) Sugar, 1/2 t (3 ml) Cornstarch, 1 t (5 ml) Rice wine, 1 T (15 ml) Oyster sauce, 1 T (15 ml)	Mix all ingredients listed. Set aside.
• Step 3. Pickling cucumbers, 3/4 lb (340 g) Garlic cloves, 3 Sugar, 1 t (5 ml) Salt, 1/4 t (1 ml) Rice vinegar, 1 t (5 ml) Hot bean paste, 1 t (5 ml)	Slice cucumbers thinly. Smash garlic to loosen skin. Discard skin and mince garlic. Mix all ingredients listed and serve.
• Step 4. Onion, 1 or 3/4 lb (340 g) from salad bar	Halve onion and cut into thin strips.
• Step 5. Cooking oil, 3 T (45 ml) Fermented black beans, 1 T (15 ml) Soy sauce	Heat wok until very hot. Add 1 T (15 ml) of oil. Add onions (Step 4), stir until soft, and then remove from wok and set aside. Pour remaining 2 T (30 ml) of oil into still hot wok, add black beans and stir briefly. Add flank steak (Step 2), and stir until almost cooked. Return onions to wok. Add soy sauce to taste and stir. Serve as soon as possible.

INGREDIENTS AND EQUIPMENT

PERISHABLES	PANTRY ITEMS		EQUIPMENT

flank steak 3/4 lb (450g)
   (ask butcher to slice thin across the
   grain)
pickling cucumbers 3/4 lb (340g)
	cornstarch
	rice wine
	rice vinegar
	cooking oil
	soy sauce
	oyster sauce
		long grain rice
		onions, any kind
		fermented black beans
		garlic
		hot bean paste
			wok or large skillet
			small rangetop
			   cassserole

NOODLES WITH SPICY BEEF SAUCE

SERVES 3 TO 4

There are noodles of noodles in Chinese grocery stores—dried noodles, fresh noodles; raw noodles, cooked noodles; noodles made from wheat, rice, soy beans, mung beans, with eggs or without..... They are available in sizes ranging from needle-thin to large sheets. I prefer the thin, dried wheat noodles which keeps on shelves and cooks in 1 1/2 minutes.

INGREDIENTS

INSTRUCTIONS

• Step 1.

Heat 2 quarts (2 liters) of water. While the water is heating, do the following:

• Step 2. Garlic, 3 cloves
Ginger, 2 slices
Hot bean paste, 1 T (15 ml)
   or to taste
Hoisin sauce, 2 T (30 ml)

Smash garlic and remove skin. Mince garlic and ginger. Combine with remaining ingredients listed.

• Step 3. Cooking oil, 2 T (30 ml)
Beef, ground, 1 1b (450 g)
Soy sauce, 1 T (15 ml)
Water, 1 C (240 ml)
Cornstarch 1 T (15 ml)

Heat wok until hot. Add oil. Add ingredients prepared in Step 2 and stir for 10 seconds. Add beef, stir until almost cooked, while at the same time adding soy sauce. Add water and bring to a boil. Turn heat to low and simmer for 5 minutes. Mix cornstarch and 1 T (15 ml) water to make paste, stir it into wok to thicken the sauce.

• Step 4. Pickling cucumbers, 2
Red bell pepper, 1
Scallions, 2

Meanwhile, julienne-cut cucumbers, by hand or with food processor. Repeat with bell pepper. Dice scallions.

• Step 5. Dried Chinese noodles,
   3/4 1b (340 g)
Bean sprouts, 2 C (480 ml)

Add noodles to boiling water prepared in Step 1. Boil 1 or 2 minutes, until *al dente*. Add bean sprouts, cook briefly, then drain. Mix noodles and bean sprouts with small amount of beef mixture (Step 3) and spread on serving platter. Garnish with cucumbers and bell pepper (Step 4). Top with remaining beef mixture. Sprinkle scallions (Step 4) on top.

• Step 6. Soy sauce
Sesame oil
Chili oil
Vinegar

Serve noodles hot or cold. Use ingredients listed as condiments. Add as much or as little as you like.

INGREDIENTS AND EQUIPMENT

PERISHABLES	PANTRY ITEMS		EQUIPMENT
gound beef 1 lb (450g)	cornstarch	hoisin sauce	wok or large skillet
pickling cucumber 2	soy sauce	cooking oil	large pot
red bell pepper 1	sesame oil	garlic	food processor
bean sprouts 2C (480ml)	chili oil	dried Chinese noodles	(optional)
scallions	rice vinegar		
fresh ginger	hot bean paste		

BEEF AND BROCCOLI IN BLACK BEAN SAUCE

SPICY BABY CORN

RICE

SERVES 3 TO 4

Stir-frying this way (as opposed to the traditional way) saves not only time and effort, but most of all, inches off your waist!

In the traditional stir-frying of meat with vegetables, the meat is first stir-fried (or even worse, oil-blanched) and set aside. Second, the vegetable is stir-fried; and third, the vegetable is combined with the meat. I blanch the vegetables in the microwave oven (without adding any oil, of course!), and then stir-fry it with the meat. You get an exciting end-product without the excess grease.

INGREDIENTS	INSTRUCTIONS
• Step 1. Flank steak, sliced, 3/4 lb (340 g) Cornstarch, 1 t (5 ml) Rice wine, 1 t (5 ml) Soy sauce, 1 T (15 ml)	Marinate steak in other ingredients listed. Set aside.
• Step 2. Rice, 1 C (240 ml) Water, 2 C (480 ml)	Wash rice. Place with water in rangetop casserole. Bring to boil over high heat. Boil uncovered for 1 minute. Turn heat to the lowest setting. Cover and simmer from 5 to 10 minutes. Keep covered until dinner time. Don't stir. As the rice cooks, do the following:
• Step 3. Baby corn, one 8 oz (230 g) can Sugar, 1 t (5 ml) Rice vinegar, 1 t (5 ml) Sesame oil, 1 t (5 ml) Chili oil, 1 t (5 ml) or to taste Salt to taste	Drain baby corn and arrange on serving platter. Mix remaining ingredients and pour over corn. Serve chilled or at room temperature.
• Step 4. Broccoli florets, 1/2 lb (230 g) Onion, 1 or 1/2 C (120 ml) if ready-cut Fermented black beans, 2 T (30 ml) Ginger, 3 slices Cooking oil, 2 T (30 ml) Water, 2 T (30 ml) Soy sauce, 1 T (15 ml)	Cut broccoli florets into bite-sized pieces. Cover and microwave on high for 2 minutes. Plunge into cold water. Drain. Chop up onion. Mince black beans and ginger. Heat wok until very hot. Swirl in oil. Add onion, black beans and ginger, stir for a few seconds. Add steak (Step 1), stir until almost cooked. Add broccoli and stir. Splash in water and soy sauce, stir. Discard ginger and serve.

INGREDIENTS AND EQUIPMENT

PERISHABLES	PANTRY ITEMS		EQUIPMENT
flank steak 3/4 lb (340g) (ask butcher to slice thin)	cornstarch	chili oil	wok or large skillet
broccoli florets 1/2 lb (230g)	rice wine	long grain rice	microwave oven
fresh ginger	cooking oil	fermented black beans	
	soy sauce	canned baby corn	
	rice vinegar	onion, any kind	
	sesame oil		

Pork

NOODLES WITH CHINESE BARBECUED PORK

SERVES 3 TO 4

"What is this? What is that?" My students who take the shopping trip to Washington's Chinatown with me are curious about everything on display. They are excited about the sight, sound and smell. They giggle like school-kids on a field trip. What always catches their eye are the long strips of reddish meat hanging behind the glass panes. It is called cha siu, or barbecued pork. It is a famous Cantonese food, marinated in hoisin sauce, soy sauce, wine, sugar, etc. and roasted in a special oven, You can eat it as is , or use it as filling for dim sum, or stir-fry it with rice, noodles, or vegetables.

INGREDIENTS	INSTRUCTIONS
• Step 1.	Bring 2 quarts (2 liters) water to a boil.
• Step 2. Snow peas, 1/4 lb (230 g) Scallions, 2	Nip ends of snow peas and remove strings. Chop up scallions.
• Step 3. Fresh Chinese noodles*, 1 lb (450 g) Sesame oil, 1 t (5 ml)	Drop noodles into boiling water prepared in Step 1. Boil until noodles are *al dente*. (Fresh noodles cook quickly. They maybe done before the water comes to boil again). Drain. Rinse in cold water. Mix with sesame oil.
• Step 4. Cooking oil, 2 T (30 ml) Chinese barbecued pork, sliced, 1/2 lb (230g)** Bean sprouts, 1/4 lb (110 g) Black pepper, a dash Soy sauce, 2 T (30 ml)	Heat wok until very hot. Add oil. Add snow peas (Step 2) and stir for 1 minute. Add pork and stir briefly. Add noodles (Step 3) and stir until heated. Add bean sprouts, pepper and soy sauce. Stir until ingredients are blended. Garnish with scallions (Step 2).
• Step 5. Soy sauce Rice vinegar Chili oil Sesame oil	Use the ingredients listed as condiments.

* Found in refrigerators at Chinese grocery stores. If not available, use fresh pasta or 3/4 1b. dried Chinese noodles. Boil the latter for 1 to 2 minutes.

** Ask the sales person to slice the pork.

INGREDIENTS AND EQUIPMENT

PERISHABLES	PANTRY ITEMS	EQUIPMENT
Chinese barbecued pork 1/2 1b (230g) (ask the storekeeper to slice) snow peas 1/4 1b (110g) bean sprouts 1/4 1b (110g) scallions fresh Chinese noodles 1 1b (450g)	cooking oil soy sauce rice vinegar chili oil sesame oil	wok or large skillet large saucepan

POT-STICKERS
EGG DROP SOUP WITH LETTUCE AND TOMATOES

SERVES 3 TO 4

There are two ways to wrap the pot-stickers: One is to have the filling completely wrapped in the wrapper, as you would do with jiaotze. The other is this quick and easy way, used in most restaurants in Taiwan.

INGREDIENTS	INSTRUCTIONS
• Step 1. Jiaotze wrappers, 1 1b (450 g)	Remove from freezer and wrap in a damp towel.
• Step 2. Frozen chopped spinach, 10 oz (280 g) package Scallions, 2 Ground pork, beef or chicken, 1 lb (450 g) Soy sauce, 1 T (15 ml) Sesame oil, 1 t (5 ml) Black pepper, a dash	Thaw spinach in microwave on low for 3 minutes. Meanwhile, chop white portion of scallions finely. Squeeze excess liquid from spinach. Mix all ingredients listed. Spread a heaping tablespoon (15 ml) of this mixture across the center of a wrapper. Moisten one edge of wrapper ① and fold it into the other. Pinch to seal but leave both ends open. Prepare the rest of the pot-stickers in this manner.
• Step 3. Chicken broth, two 14 oz (400 g) cans Water, 1 C (240 ml)	Combine broth and water in sauce pan over medium heat. Meanwhile, do the following:
• Step 4. Cooking oil, 1 T (15 ml) Water, 1/2 C (120 ml) Soy sauce Rice vinegar Chili oil	Heat large skillet over medium heat. Add oil. Set pot-stickers in rows in skillet, sides touching. ② Fry until bottoms turn crusty. Add water, cover and simmer until most liquid is absorbed, about 6 minutes. Put pot-stickers on serving platter, bottom sides up. Serve with soy sauce, vinegar and oil as condiments.
• Step 5. Egg, 1 Lettuce leaves Tomato, 1 Vinegar, a dash Black pepper, a dash	Beat egg. Tear lettuce into smaller pieces. Cut tomato into wedges and drop into boiling broth prepared in Step 3. Boil for 1 minute. Add lettuce. When it returns to a boil, turn off heat. Dribble egg in slowly while gently stirring. Add a dash of vinegar and pepper.

①    ②

INGREDIENTS AND EQUIPMENT

PERISHABLES
coarsely ground pork, beef or chicken 1 lb (450g) package
frozen chopped spinach one 10oz (280g) package
leafy lettuce, any green variety
tomato 1
eggs
jiaotze wrappers 1 lb (450g)
scallions

PANTRY ITEMS
soy sauce
cooking oil
sesame oil
chili oil (optional)
rice vinegar
chicken broth, canned

EQUIPMENT
large skillet with cover
medium saucepan
microwave oven

SOUPY NOODLES WITH PORK AND SICHUAN VEGETABLE

This is a favorite Chinese lunch. Broccoli is a relatively recent import into Taiwan. I have modified the traditional dish by adding broccoli to provide some color and fiber.

A soupy noodle dish consists of three components: the noodles, the soup and the topping.

INGREDIENTS	INSTRUCTIONS
• Step 1. Pork, pre-sliced, 3/4 lb (340 g) Cornstarch, 1 t (5 ml) Rice wine, 1 t (5 ml) Soy sauce, 1 T (15 ml)	Mix ingredients listed and let stand at room temperature.
• Step 2.	Bring 2 quarts (2 liters) water to a boil in a large pot.
• Step 3. Scallion, 1 Broccoli florets, 1/4 lb (110 g)	Dice scallion. Cut broccoli florets into bite-sized pieces.
• Step 4. Beef broth, one 14 oz (400 g) can Water, 1 C (240 ml)	Combine broth and water and bring to a boil in a small pot.
• Step 5. Sichuan vegetable, shredded, 1/2 C (120 ml) Cooking oil, 2 T (30 ml) Rice wine, 1 T (15 ml)	Heat wok until very hot. As wok heats, rinse Sichuan vegetable. Add oil to wok. Add Sichuan vegetable and stir. Add pork (Step 1) and stir until cooked. Add wine. Stir briefly, then set aside.
• Step 6. Fresh Chinese noodles,* 1 lb (450 g) Sesame oil, 1 t (5 ml)	Add noodles to large pot of boiling water prepared in Step 2. Boil until cooked, about 10 seconds. Drain. Mix with sesame oil and place in soup tureen.
• Step 7.	Drop broccoli (Step 3) in boiling broth prepared in Step 4. Boil for 30 seconds. Pour into soup tureen containing noodles. Add pork (Step 5) and garnish with scallion (Step 3).

* Found in refrigerators at Chinese grocery stores. If not available, use fresh pasta or 3/4 1b. dried Chinese noodles. Boil the latter for 1 to 2 minutes.

INGREDIENTS AND EQUIPMENT

PERISHABLES	PANTRY ITEMS	EQUIPMENT
pork 3/4 lb (340g) (ask butcher to cut into thin strips) broccoli florets 1/4 lb (110g) scallion fresh Chinese noodles 1 lb (450g)	cornstarch cooking oil sesame oil rice wine soy sauce shredded Sichuan vegetable canned beef broth	wok or large skillet microwaveabl small pot

PORK AND RICE CASSEROLE

SERVES 2 TO 3

"Can I substitute ground chicken for ground pork or beef?" Certainly you can. You can even use sliced chicken in place of other sliced meat, in most cases. The only difference, besides the taste and fat content, is that chicken and beef get tough more easily than pork.

INGREDIENTS	INSTRUCTIONS
• Step 1. Rice, 3/4 C (180 ml) Water, 1 1/2 C (360 ml)	Wash rice. Place along with water in microwave-safe casserole dish. Cover and microwave on high for 4 minutes. Rotate, uncover and microwave on high until most water is absorbed, about 7 minutes.
• Step 2. Pork, ground, 3/4 lb (340 g) Salt, 1/2 t (3 ml) Cornstarch, 1 t (5 ml) Rice wine, 1 T (15 ml) Soy sauce, 2 T (30 ml) Sesame oil, 1 t (5 ml) Ginger, 3 slices	Mix all ingredients listed. Set aside.
• Step 3. Tomato, 1 Water chestnuts, one 8 oz (230 g) can Asparagus, 1/2 lb (230 g) Scallion, 1	Cut tomato into wedges. Drain water chestnuts and chop coarsely. Mix tomato and water chestnuts with pork (Step 2). Place mixture on top of rice in casserole dish (Step 1). Cover and microwave on high for 5 minutes. Meanwhile, remove tough bottom ends of asparagus. Cut into 1 1/2 inch (4 cm) sections and mix with pork mixture without disturbing rice. Discard ginger. Cover and microwave on high until pork is cooked, about 2 minutes. Remove cover. Dice scallion and garnish the casserole.
• Step 4. Side dishes (optional)	Select one or more pungent relishes such as Soy Sauce Cucumbers (p.140) or Fried Fish Paste (p.137) to complement this delicate-tasting dish.

INGREDIENTS AND EQUIPMENT

PERISHABLES	PANTRY ITEMS	EQUIPMENT
ground pork 3/4 lb (340g)	cornstarch	microwave oven
tomato 1	rice wine	microwaveable casserole
asparagus 1/2 lb (230g)	soy sauce	
fresh ginger	sesame oil	
scallions	long grain rice	
	water chestnuts	

SAUSAGE AND RICE CASSEROLE

SERVES 3 TO 4

Traditionally, Chinese sausages are made of pork, pork liver or duck liver. There are "low fat" varieties made of lean pork and chicken meat now available. However, they are not as tasty as the old-fashioned sausages.

INGREDIENTS

INSTRUCTIONS

- **Step 1.** Rice, 1 C (240 ml)
  Water, 2 1/4 C (660 ml)

  Wash rice. Place along with water in a microwave-safe casserole dish. Cover and microwave on high for 5 minutes. Rotate, uncover and microwave on high until most water is absorbed, about 7 minutes.

- **Step 2.** Pork or chicken, sliced,
  3/4 lb (340 g)
  Cornstarch, 1 t (5 ml)
  Rice wine, 1 T (15 ml)
  Soy sauce, 1 T (15 ml)
  Sesame oil, 1 t (5 ml)
  Ginger, 3 slices

  Mix ingredients listed. Set aside.

- **Step 3.** Black mushrooms, one
  8 oz (230 g) can
  Water chestnuts, sliced,
  one 6 oz (170 g) can
  Chinese pork sausages, 4

  Drain mushrooms and water chestnuts. Slice sausages. Spread meat mixture (Step 2) over top of rice in casserole dish. Next, add layers of mushrooms, water chestnuts and sausages. Cover and microwave on high for 4 minutes. Rotate and microwave 5 more minutes.

- **Step 4.** Snow peas, 1/4 lb (110 g)

  Nip ends of snow peas and remove strings. Mix snow peas with the meat and vegetables in the casserole without distrubing the rice. Break apart any pieces of meat that are stuck together. Cover and microwave on high until meat is fully cooked, about 2 minutes. Uncover so that the snow peas won't yellow. Discard ginger.

- **Step 5.** Scallion, 1
  Side dishes (optional)

  Dice scallion, sprinkle over top of casserole. Serve with one or more relishes such as shredded fish (p.140) or Soy Sauce Cucumbers (p.140).

INGREDIENTS AND EQUIPMENT

PERISHABLES	PANTRY ITEMS	EQUIPMENT
Chinese pork sausage 4	cornstarch	microwaveable casserole
pork or chicken 3/4 lb (340g)	rice wine	microwave oven
(ask butcher to slice thin)	soy sauce	
snow peas 1/4 lb (110g)	sesame oil	
fresh ginger	long grain rice	
scallions	sliced water chestnuts	
	canned black mushrooms	

PORK WITH FRESH RICE NOODLES

SERVES 2 TO 3

Fesh rice noodles, (sha ho fen) are sold ready-cooked, either in large sheets or broad strips; found in refrigerators at Chinese grocery stores. Shanghai choy is a small variety of bok choy. The stems are light green. Even the outer leaves are tender, therefore there is very little waste.

INGREDIENTS

INSTRUCTIONS

- Step 1. Pork, sliced, 3/4 lb (340 g)
  Cornstarch, 1 t (5 ml)
  Oyster sauce, 1 T (15 ml)
  Rice wine, 1 t (5 ml)
  Black pepper, a dash

  Mix all ingredients listed. Let stand at room temperature.

- Step 2. Carrot, 1, or 1/2 C (120 ml)
    ready-shredded
  Shanghai choy, 3 stalks
  Scallion, 1

  Peel and julienne-cut the carrot. Wash Shanghai choy and cut them into bite-sized pieces. Dice scallion.

- Step 3. Fresh rice noodles, 12 oz (340 g)
  Cooking oil, 2 T (30 ml)
  Bamboo shoots, sliced
    and canned, 1/2 C (120 ml)
  Soy sauce to taste

  Heat wok until very hot. As wok heats, separate noodles. Add oil to wok. Add pork (Step 1) and stir until it changes color. Add bamboo shoots and carrot (Step 2), stir briefly. Add noodles, stir until heated. Add Shanghai choy (Step 2) and scallions (Step 2), sprinkle with soy sauce, and transfer to a serving platter.

- Step 4. Soy sauce
  Sesame oil
  Chili oil

  Use ingredients listed as condiments.

INGREDIENTS AND EQUIPMENT

PERISHABLES	PANTRY ITEMS	EQUIPMENT
pork, butt or boneless loin 3/4 1b (340g) (ask butcher to slice thin)	cornstarch	wok or large skillet
Shanghai choy 3 stalks	soy sauce	
fresh rice noodles 12 oz (340g)	oyster sauce	
carrots	sesame oil	
scallions	chili oil	
	rice wine	
	cooking oil	
	bamboo shoots, pre-sliced	

STUFFED ZUCCHINI

SHREDDED CARROTS WITH CURRY DRESSING

RICE

SERVES 2 TO 3

This is one of the menus that can be doubled, unlike the stir-fried dishes that will taste steamed if doubled. If you are speedy, you can still do the double in 30 minutes. Halving the zucchini lengthwise makes the stuffing process a lot faster.

INGREDIENTS	INSTRUCTIONS
• Step 1. Rice, 3/4 C (180 ml) Water, 1 1/2 C (360 ml)	Wash rice. Place with water in rangetop casserole. Bring to boil over high heat. Boil uncovered for 1 minute. Turn heat to the lowest setting. Cover and simmer anywhere from 5 to 15 minutes. Keep covered until dinner time. Don't stir. As the rice cooks, do the following:
• Step 2. Small zucchini, 3 Cornstarch	Halve zucchini lengthwise. Scoop out the center with a spoon. (Eat what you have scooped out now—of course, that's the cook's prerogative!) Dust and smear inside lightly with cornstarch.
• Step 3. Scallion, 1 Water chestnuts, canned, 6-8 Coarsely ground pork, 1/2 lb (230 g) Rice wine, 1 t (5 ml) Oyster sauce, 1 T (15 ml) Cornstarch, 1 T (15 ml) Black pepper, a dash	Dice white portion of scallion. Coarsely chop up water chestnuts. Combine all ingredients listed. Use mixture to stuff hollow portion of zucchini (Step 2).
• Step 4. Cooking oil, 1 T (15 ml) Canned broth, any kind, 1 C (240 ml)	Heat skillet until very hot. Add oil. Swirl to spread evenly. Over medium heat, fry stuffed side of zucchini until slightly browned. Turn on other side and repeat. Add broth. Bring to a boil, cover and simmer for 6 minutes. Serve hot.
• Step 5. Curry powder, 2 t (5 ml) Rice vinegar, 1 T (15 ml) Sesame oil, 1 t (5 ml) Salt to taste Carrots shredded, 1/2 lb (230 g)	As zucchini simmers, mix curry powder with vinegar. Next, add sesame oil and salt. Pour mixture over carrots and toss. Serve chilled or at room temperature.

INGREDIENTS AND EQUIPMENT

PERISHABLES	PANTRY ITEMS		EQUIPMENT
coarsely ground pork 1/2 1b (230g) small zucchini 3 shredded carrots from salad bar 1/2 1b (230g) scallions	cornstarch cooking oil rice vinegar rice wine sesame oil	oyster sauce canned broth canned water chestnuts long grain rice curry powder	small rangetop casserole skillet with cover

PORK CHOPS IN HOISIN SAUCE

CURRIED MIXED VEGETABLES

SCALLION ROLLS

SERVES 4

Look Mom, no chopping! If you don't want to cook the three-course meal, you can choose to cook only Pork Chops Hoisin Sauce, printed on   ; Curried Mixed Vegetables, printed on

INGREDIENTS

INSTRUCTIONS

• Step 1. Scallion rolls, 4	Take scallion rolls out of freezer and wrap in damp towel.

• Step 2.
Onion, 1/2 or 1 C ready-shredded
Cooking oil, 1 T (15 ml)
Dried chilies, 3
Frozen mixed vegetables, 1 lb (450 g)
Curry powder, 1 T (15 ml)
Salt, 1/2 t (3ml)
Water, 2 T (30 ml)
Soy sauce

Chop onion. Heat wok until very hot. Add oil. Add chilies and stir for 10 seconds. Add onion and stir for 1 minute. Add mixed vegetables. Stir until thawed and warm while at the same time adding the curry powder and salt. Add water. Keep stirring over high heat until fully cooked, about 2 minutes. Correct the seasoning with soy sauce and serve.

• Step 3.
Pork chops, thin, 4-6
Salt, 1/2 t (3ml)
Black pepper, a dash
Cornstarch, 1 t (5 ml)
Rice wine, 1 t (5 ml)
Soy sauce, 1 T (15 ml)

Pound pork chops with back of cleaver. Mix the remaining ingredients and rub on pork chops.

• Step 4.
Scallions, 2
Cooking oil, 1 T (15 ml)
Ginger, 3 slices
Hoisin sauce, 1 T (15 ml)
Soy sauce, 1 T (15 ml)
Ketchup, 2 T (30 ml)
Broth or water, 6 T (90 ml)

Heat skillet over medium heat. As skillet heats, cut scallions into bite-sized sections. Add oil to skillet and swirl to spread evenly. Brown both sides of pork chops. Push chops to side of skillet and add scallions and ginger, stir for 1/2 minute. Return chops to center of skillet, add remaining ingredients listed. Bring to a boil, cover and simmer until chops are fully cooked, about 5 minutes. Turn occasionally. Discard ginger before serving.

• Step 5.

Microwave scallion rolls (Step 1), still wrapped in towel, on high for 1 to 3 minutes, depending on the size and how well they have been thawed. Serve hot.

INGREDIENTS AND EQUIPMENT

PERISHABLES	PANTRY ITEMS		EQUIPMENT
thin pork chops 4-6	cornstarch	curry powder	wok
frozen mixed vegetables 1 1b (450g)	cooking oil	dried chilies	skillet with cover
shredded onions 1 C (240ml)	ketchup		
scallions	rice wine		
fresh ginger	soy sauce		
scallion rolls	hoisin sauce		

Fish

WHOLE FISH IN HOT BEAN SAUCE

STIR-FRIED BROCCOLI

RICE

SERVES 3 TO 4

*Kctchup in a Chinese dish? No kidding! It's not American hamburgers, you know?
Yes, the Chinese do use ketchup in many dishes. Ketchup with hot bean paste, garlic
and ginger is dynamite!*

	INGREDIENTS	INSTRUCTIONS
• Step 1.	Whole fish, 1 1/2 lb to 2 lb (680 to 900 g) Salt, 1/2 t (3 ml)	Rub salt over fish. Place on oval microwave-safe platter. Set aside.
• Step 2.	Rice, 1 C (240 ml) Water, 2 C (480 ml)	Wash rice. Place with water in a rangetop casserole. Bring to boil over high heat. Boil uncovered for 1 minute. Turn heat to the lowest setting. Cover and simmer anywhere between 5 to 15 miuntes. Let stay covered until dinner is served. Don't stir.
• Step 3.	Garlic cloves, 6 Ginger, 6 slices Hot bean paste, 1 T (15 ml), or to taste	Smash garlic to loosen skin. Remove skin. Mince garlic and ginger. Combine with hot bean paste.
• Step 4.	Cooking oil, 1 T (15 ml) Rice wine, 2 T (30 ml) Sugar, 4 t (20 ml) Soy sauce, 2 T (30 ml) Ketchup, 6 T (90 ml) Water, 1/4 C (60 ml) Cornstarch, 1 T (15 ml) Water, 1 T (15 ml)	Heat wok or sauce pan until hot. Add oil. Add mixture from Step 3 and stir until fragrant. Add wine. Reduce heat. Add sugar, soy sauce, ketchup and water. Bring to boil. Mix cornstarch with water to make a paste. Stir paste slowly into mixture until it is slightly thickened. Discard the remaining paste.
• Step 5.	Scallion, 1	Pour sauce prepared in Step 4 over fish (Step 1). Cover and microwave* on high for 4 minutes. Rotate and repeat. While the fish is cooking, dice the scallion. Use it as a garnish.
• Step 6.	Broccoli florets, 3/4 lb (340 g) Cooking oil, 2 T (30 ml) Rice wine, 1 T (15 ml) Vinegar, 1 t (5 ml) Salt, a dash Pepper, a dash	Cut broccoli florets into bite-sized pieces. Heat wok until very hot. Swirl oil in. Add broccoli. Stir for 2 to 3 minutes. Add wine and vinegar. Add salt and pepper to season. Stir briefly and serve.

* If the carrousel does not rotate when you place the fish on it, turn the oven tray upside down.

INGREDIENTS AND EQUIPMENT

PERISHABLES	PANTRY ITEMS		EQUIPMENT
whole fish 1 1/2-2 lb (680-900g), any with white meat	cornstarch	rice vinegar	microwave oven
broccoli florets 3/4 lb (340g)	soy sauce	hot bean paste	wok or sauce pan
fresh ginger	garlic	ketchup	rangetop casserole
scallions	cooking oil	rice	
	rice wine		

FISH AND PEPPERS WITH BLACK BEANS

SWEET AND SOUR LOTUS ROOTS

RICE

SERVES 2 TO 3

The Chinese use lotus not only in poetry and painting, but also in cooking: the roots are stewed or stir-fried, leaves are used to wrap rice and meats, and the nutty tasting seeds are used in sweets.

INGREDIENTS	INSTRUCTIONS
• Step 1. Fish fillet, 3/4 lb (340 g) Cornstarch, 1 t (5 ml) Rice wine, 1 t (5 ml) Soy sauce, 1 T (15 ml)	Cut fish into thick slices. Mix with remaining ingredients. Set aside.
• Step 2. Rice, 3/4 C (180 ml) Water, 1 1/2 C (360 ml)	Wash rice. Place with water in a rangetop casserole. Bring to boil over high heat. Boil for 1 minute, uncovered. Turn heat to the lowest setting, cover and simmer for 5 to 10 minutes. If the pot boils over, keep the lid ajar for 2 to 3 minutes, then put the lid back on until dinner time. Don't stir. While the rice cooks, do the following:
• Step 3. Lotus root, 1 lb (450 g) Cooking oil, 2 T (30 ml) Red wine vinegar, 2 T (30 ml) Sugar, 2 T (30 ml) Salt	Cut off both ends of lotus root. Slice thinly. Heat wok until very hot. Add oil, then add lotus root, stir for 1 minute. Add vinegar and sugar and stir for 2 minutes. Season with salt. Serve chilled or at room temperature.
• Step 4. Bell peppers, 3/4 lb (340 g) Scallions, 2 Cooking oil, 2 T (30 ml) Fermented black beans, 2 T (30 ml) Ginger, 3 slices Rice wine, 1 T (15 ml) Soy sauce to taste	Cut peppers into bite-sized pieces. Sprinkle with a little water, microwave on high for 2 minutes. Heat wok until very hot. As wok heats, dice scallions. Add oil to wok. Add black beans and ginger and stir for 10 seconds. Add fish (Step 1) and stir gently until it becomes opaque. Add peppers and stir briefly. Add wine, soy sauce and stir. Discard ginger. Garnish with scallions.

INGREDIENTS AND EQUIPMENT

PERISHABLES	PANTRY ITEMS	EQUIPMENT
fish fillet, any with firm meat 3/4 lb (340g) lotus root 1 lb (450g) peppers 2 scallions fresh ginger	cornstarch cooking oil rice wine soy sauce fermented black beans long grain rice red wine vinegar	wok or large skillet small rangetop casserole microwave oven

SICHUAN STIR-FRIED FISH SLICES

BROCCOLI AND TOMATO SALAD

RICE

SERVES 2 TO 3

It takes so little time to arrange this salad with so much effect.

INGREDIENTS	INSTRUCTIONS
• Step 1. Fish fillet, 3/4 lb (340 g) Cornstarch, 1 t (5 ml) Rice wine, 1 t (5 ml)	Cut fish into thick slices (choose a fish with firm meat). Marinate slices in mixture of cornstarch and rice wine.
• Step 2. Rice, 3/4 C (180 ml) Water, 1 1/2 C (360 ml)	Wash rice. Place with water in a rangetop casserole. Bring to boil over high heat. Boil uncovered for 1 minute. Turn heat to the lowest setting, cover and simmer anywhere between 5 to 10 minutes. Let stay covered until dinner is served. Don't stir.
• Step 3. Broccoli florets, 1/2 lb (230 g) Tomato, 2 Salt, 1/2 t (3 ml) Sugar, 1 t (5 ml) Sesame oil, 1 t (5 ml) Rice vinegar, 1 T (15 ml)	Cut broccoli florets into bite-sized pieces. Place on plate, sprinkle with water, cover and microwave on high for 1 1/2 minutes. Plunge into pan of cold water. Drain and place on center of serving platter. Slice tomatoes and arrange slices along edge of platter. Mix remaining ingredients and pour over vegetables before serving. Serve chilled.
• Step 4. Sichuan vegetable, 1/2 C (120 ml) Garlic, 3 cloves Cooking oil, 2 T (30 ml) Sugar, 1 t (5 ml)	Rinse Sichuan vegetable. Smash garlic to loosen and discard skin. Mince garlic. Heat wok until very hot. Add oil. Stir in garlic and Sichuan vegetable. Add fish (Step 1) and stir gently until color becomes opaque while at the same time adding sugar. Serve hot.

INGREDIENTS AND EQUIPMENT

PERISHABLES	PANTRY ITEMS	EQUIPMENT
fish fillet, any kind with firm meat 3/4 lb (340 g) broccoli florets 1/2 lb (230g) tomatoes 2	cornstarch rice wine rice vinegar cooking oil sesame oil shredded Suchuan vegetable garlic rice	wok or large skillet microwave oven

SOUR AND HOT FISH CHOWDER

PRESSED TOFU WITH CHINESE CHIVES

STEAMED BUNS

SERVES 4 TO 6

Chinese chives look almost like grass that has not been mowed during a long vacation. Very fragrant to those who like it, but smelly to those who don't. Just sniff and decide which group you belong to.

INGREDIENTS	INSTRUCTIONS
• Step 1. Steamed buns, 8 Wood ears, 1/4 C (60 ml)	Remove steamed buns from freezer and wrap in damp towel. Soak wood ears in warm water.
• Step 2. Fish fillet, 1 lb (450 g) Ginger, 1 thick slice Salt, 1/2 t (3 ml)	Dice fish. Use a garlic press to squeeze juice from ginger slice directly onto fish. Add salt and mix.
• Step 3. Chilies, 2 Brown pressed tofu, 1 lb (450 g) Chinese chives, 1/2 lb (230 g) Cooking oil, 2 T (30 ml) Fermented black beans, 1 T (15 ml) Soy sauce to taste	Cut chilies open, rinse away seeds and shred. Shred tofu, cut chives into small sections. Heat wok until hot. Add oil. Add black beans and stir for 10 seconds. Add tofu, stir for 1 minute. Add chives, stir for 1 minute. Add soy sauce only if needed. Serve hot or cold.
• Step 4.	Microwave steamed buns, still wrapped in towel, on high for 2 to 4 minutes, depending on the size and how much they have been thawed.
• Step 5. Chicken broth, two 12 oz (400 g) cans Water, 3 C (720 ml)	Combine broth and water and bring to a boil.

• Step 6. Smithfield ham, a small
  piece (optional)
Water chestnuts, 1 C (240 ml)
Frozen green peas,
  1 C (240 ml)
White pepper, 1 t (5 ml)
Sugar, 1 t (5 ml)
Rice vinegar, 2 T (30 ml)
Soy sauce, 1 t (5ml) or to taste
	Mince ham and dice water chestnuts. Drain wood ears (Step 1). Mix pepper, sugar, vinegar and soy sauce to create a seasoning. Add ingredients to boiling broth (Step 5) in the following order, stir and bring to boil again each time you add: wood ears, water chestnuts, green peas, fish (Step 2), and seasoning.

• Step 7. Cornstarch, 3 T (45 ml) Water, 3 T (45 ml) Egg whites, 2	Mix cornstarch with water to form a paste. Add to soup prepared in Step 6 slowly while stirring. Turn off heat. Beat egg whites and dribble into the soup, stirring at the same time. Pour soup into tureen and garnish with ham in Step 6.

INGREDIENTS AND EQUIPMENT

PERISHABLES	PANTRY ITEMS	EQUIPMENT
fish fillet 1 lb (450g)	white pepper	rangetop casserole
brown pressed tofu 1 lb (450g)	cornstarch	wok or skillet
chinese chives 1/2 lb (230g)	rice vinegar	microwave oven
steamed buns	cooking oil	
fresh ginger	soy sauce	
eggs	wood ears	
Smithfield ham (optional)	chicken broth	
chilies 2	fermented black beans	
frozen peas	water chestnuts	

SPICY NOODLES WITH FISH SLICES

You always tell me to "Heat wok on high heat; As wok heats, do this and that.... I am afraid by the time I am ready to pour in the oil, there might be a fire! " Wait a minutes, don't rush to call the fire department. Nothing can happen to the wok if it is a good, old-fashioned wok (see p.145). The wok must be very hot before you start stir-frying. It can only be under-heated, rarely over-heated.

INGREDIENTS	INSTRUCTIONS
• Step 1.	Bring 2 quarts (2 liters) of water to a boil.
• Step 2. Fish fillet, 3/4 lb (340 g) Salt, 1/2 t (3 ml) Cornstarch, 1 t (5 ml) Rice wine, 1 t (5 ml)	Cut fish into large slices. Mix with remaining ingredients listed. Set aside.
• Step 3. Spinach leaves, 1/2 lb (230 g)	Wash spinach. Discard tough stems. Tear leaves into smaller pieces.
• Step 4. Garlic, 3 colves Ginger, 3 slices Hot bean paste, 1 t (5 ml) or to taste	Smash garlic to loosen and remove skin. Mince garlic and ginger. Combine all ingredients.
• Step 5. Chinese dried noodles, 1/2 lb (230 g) Sesame oil, 1 t (5 ml)	Add noodles to pot of boiling water prepared in Step 1. Boil noodles until *al dente*, about 1 to 2 minutes. Drain and rinse with cold water to cool. Mix with sesame oil.
• Step 6. Scallions, 2 Cooking oil, 2 T (30 ml) Soy sauce	Heat wok until very hot. As wok heats, dice scallions. Add oil to wok. Stir in seasoning prepared in Step 4. Add fish (Step 2) and stir gently until fish is almost all opaque. Add noodles (Step 5), stir gently until heated. Add spinach (Step 3), stir briefly. Season with soy sauce. Transfer to a serving platter and garnish with scallions.
• Step 7. Soy sauce Chili oil Rice vinegar	Use the ingredietns listed as condiments.

INGREDIENTS AND EQUIPMENT

PERISHABLES	PANTRY ITEMS		EQUIPMENT
fish fillet, any with firm meat 3/4 lb (340g)	cornstarch	soy sauce	wok or large skillet
spinach leaves 1/2 lb (230g)	garlic	chili oil	large pot
scallions	rice wine	hot bean paste	colander
fresh ginger	cooking oil	sesame oil	
	rice vinegar	dried Chinese noodles, thin variety	

FISH FILLET WITH SICHUAN VEGETABLE

PEPPERS WITH BLACK BEANS

RICE WITH SESAME SEEDS

SERVES 2 TO 3

Sichuan vegetables are sold in cans at Chinese grocery stores. They are knobby stems of mustard green preserved in salt and chili powder. Used mostly as a spice for Sichuan and Hunan cooking, they add a unique spicy flavor and aroma to anything you cook.

INGREDIENTS	INSTRUCTIONS
• Step 1. Fish fillet, 3/4 lb (340 g) Sichuan vegetable, 1/2 C (120 ml) Rice wine, 1 T (15 ml) Sesame oil, 1 t (5 ml) Cooking oil, 1 T (15 ml), optional	Place fillet on microwave-safe platter, with thicker pieces toward the edge of platter. Rinse Sichuan vegetable in water. Mix with remaining ingredients listed and spread over fish. Set aside.
• Step 2. Rice, 3/4 C (180 ml) Water, 1 1/2 C (360 ml) Black sesame seeds, 1 T (15 ml)	Wash rice. Place with water in a rangetop casserole. Bring to boil over high heat. Boil uncovered for 1 minute. Turn heat to the lowest setting, cover and simmer for 5 to 10 minutes. Keep covered until dinner time. Don't stir. Garnish with sesame seeds before serving. While the rice cooks, do the following:

• Step 3. Bell peppers, 3 or 3/4 lb (340 g)
    from salad bar
Fermented black beans,
    1 T (15 ml)
	Cut peppers into julienne strips. Rinse black beans.

• Step 4. Cilantro or chopped scallion	Cover fish (Step 1) and microwave on high for 3 to 4 minutes. Rotate and repeat. The fish is done when opaque. Check by poking a piece in the center of plate. Rearrange Sichuan vegetable to cover the spot. Garnish with cilantro.
• Step 5. Garlic, 3 cloves Cooking oil, 2 T (30 ml) Soy sauce, 1 t (5 ml) or to taste	Meanwhile, heat wok until very hot. While wok is heating, remove skin from garlic. Mince garlic. Add oil to wok. Add black beans (Step 3) and garlic and stir for 10 seconds. Add bell peppers (Step 3) and stir for 2 minutes. Sprinkle on soy sauce, stir briefly, and serve.

INGREDIENTS AND EQUIPMENT

PERISHABLES
fish fillet, any kind 3/4 lb (340g)
bell pepper of any color 2-3 or
    3/4 lb (340g) from salad bar
cilantro or scallion

PANTRY ITEMS
rice wine
soy sauce
cooking oil
sesame oil
shredded Sichuan vegetable
long grain rice
fermented black beans
black sesame seeds

EQUIPMENT
wok or large skillet
rangetop casserole
microwave oven

PAN-FRIED FISH FILLET

BROCCOLI AND CARROTS WITH OYSTER DRESSING

STEAMED BUNS

SERVES 3 TO 4

This fish dish is one that all my students, friends and relatives are raving about! If you want to make only this dish, just follow the text printed on

INGREDIENTS	INSTRUCTIONS
• Step 1. Steamed buns, 8	Remove buns from freezer and wrap in damp towel.
• Step 2. Fish fillet, 1 1b (450 g) Salt, 1/2 t (3 ml)	Rub salt over fish. Let stand at room temperature.
• Step 3. Carrots, 2 Broccoli florets, 1/2 1b (230 g) Sugar, 1 t (5 ml) Oyster sauce, 2 t (10 ml) Soy sauce, 2 t (10 ml) Water, 1 T (15 ml) Sesame oil, 2 t (10 ml) Salt to taste	Peel and slice carrots. Sprinkle with a little bit of water. Cover and microwave on high for 1 minute. Arrange around serving platter. Cut the brocccoli florets into bite-sized pieces. Sprinkle with a little bit of water, cover and microwave on high for 1 1/2 minutes. Plunge into cold water to cool. Drain and place on center of platter containing carrots. Mix remaining ingredients listed and pour over the carrots and broccoli before serving. Serve chilled or at room temperature.
• Step 4. Garlic, 3 cloves Ginger, 1 thick slice Scallion, 1 Sugar, 1 T (15 ml) Soy sauce, 2 T (30 ml) Rice vinegar, 2 T (30 ml) Water, 1 T (15 ml) Sesame oil, 1 t (5 ml)	Remove skin from garlic. Mince garlic and ginger. Dice scallion. Combine all ingredients to make a seasoning.
• Step 5. Flour, 1/2 C Cooking oil, 2 T (30 ml)	Shake fish pieces (Step 2) in flour in a bag, one at a time. Shake off excess flour. Heat oil in skillet and brown both sides of fillet over medium heat. Transfer onto serving platter. Add seasoning prepared in Step 4 and serve.
• Step 6.	Start preparing steamed buns (Step 1) before fish is fully cooked. Place buns, still wrapped in towel, in microwave and cook on high for 1 to 3 minutes.

INGREDIENTS AND EQUIPMENT

PERISHABLES	PANTRY ITEMS	EQUIPMENT
fish fillet, any kind with firm meat, 1 1b (450g) broccoli florets 1/2 1b (230g) carrots steamed buns fresh ginger scallions	soy sauce cooking oil oyster sauce sesame oil rice vinegar garlic all-purpose flour	large skillet microwave oven

FISH STEAKS IN HOT BEAN SAUCE

SOY BEANS WITH RED-IN-SNOW

RICE WITH SESAME SEEDS

SERVES 2 TO 3

Red-in-snow is a green leafy vegetable which comes up very early in the spring. Its root is red and often visible in the snow. It is available preserved in cans. It is yum yum delicious when cooked with meat, peas or beans.

INGREDIENTS	INSTRUCTIONS
• Step 1. Rice, 3/4 C (180 ml) Water, 1 1/2 C (360 ml) Black sesame seeds, 1 T (15 ml)	Wash rice. Place with water in a rangetop casserole. Bring to boil over high heat. Boil uncovered for 1 minute. Turn heat to the lowest setting. Cover and simmer anywhere from 5 to 15 minutes. Keep covered until dinner time. Don't stir. Garnish with sesame before serving.
• Step 2. Garlic, 3 cloves Ginger, 3 slices Cornstarch, 1 T (15 ml) Rice wine, 1 T (15 ml) Hot bean paste, 1 t (5 ml) or to taste Ketchup, 2 T (30 ml) Soy sauce, 2 T (30 ml) Water, 1/2 C (120 ml) Cooking oil, 1 T (15 ml), optional	Meanwhile, smash garlic to loosen skin. Remove skin. Mince garlic along with ginger. Combine all ingredients listed in microwave-safe bowl. Cover and microwave on high for 1 minute. Stir and repeat.
• Step 3. Fish steak or fillet, 3/4 lb(340 g) Cilantro or diced scallion	Place fish steak on shallow microwave-safe dish. Spread sauce prepared in Step 2 over fish. Cover and microwave on high for 2 to 3 minutes. Rotate and repeat. Let stand for 2 minutes. The fish is done when opaque. Check by poking a piece in the center of plate. Cover the spot with cilantro.
• Step 4. Red-in-snow, 1 small can Cooking oil, 1 T (15 ml) Sesame oil, 1 t (5 ml) Frozen soy beans, 1 lb (450 g) Sugar, 1 t (5 ml) Soy sauce to taste	While the fish is cooking, heat wok until very hot. Rinse red-in-snow in water and squeeze out excess moisture. Add cooking and sesame oil to wok. Add red-on-snow and cook for 1 minute. Add soy beans and stir until they are fully cooked, about 2 minutes. Meanwhile, add sugar. If necessary, sprinkle on a little water. Sesaon with soy sauce.

INGREDIENTS AND UTENSILS

PERISHABLES	PANTRY ITEMS		EQUIPMENT
fish steaks or fillet 3/4 lb (340g)	cornstarch	hot bean paste	microwave oven
frozen soy beans 1 lb (340g)	garlic	sesame oil	small rangetop casserole
scallions	rice wine	ketchup	wok or skillet
fresh ginger	cooking oil	long grain rice	
cilantro or scallions	soy sauce	black sesame	

SPICY WHOLE FISH WITH BLACK BEANS

ASPARAGUS AND BABY CORN

RICE

SERVES 2 TO 3

For Chinese New Year celebrations, a fish, Yu, is a must. Phonetically, Yu sounds like "surplus" which requires "savings". But even a spendthrift American is quite welcome to a delicious fish like this one!

INGREDIENTS	INSTRUCTIONS
• Step 1. Whole fish, 1 to 1 1/2 lb (450 to 680 g) Salt, 1/2 t (3 ml) Rice wine, 1 t (5 ml)	Place fish on oval microwave-safe platter. Rub on mixture of salt and wine.
• Step 2. Rice, 3/4 C (180 ml) Water, 1 1/2 C (360 ml)	Wash rice. Place with water in a rangetop casserole. Bring to boil over high heat. Boil for 1 minute, uncovered. Turn heat to the lowest setting, cover and simmer for 5 to 10 minutes. Keep covered until dinner time. Don't stir. While the rice cooks, do the following:
• Step 3. Ginger, 6 thin slices Fresh chilies, 3 Fermented black beans, 2 T (30 ml) Soy sauce, 1 T (15 ml) Rice wine, 1 T (15 ml) Sesame oil, 1 T (15 ml) Scallions, 2	Shred ginger. Slice chilies diagonally and rinse away seeds. Rinse black beans. Mix all ingredients listed except scallions and pour over fish (Step 1). Cover and micorwave* on high for 3 minutes. Rotate and repeat. Meanwhile, shred scallions. Check center of fish to make sure it is fully cooked. If so, garnish with scallion shreds and serve.
• Step 4. Asparagus, 1 1b (450 g) Baby corn, one 15 oz (450 g) can Cooking oil, 2 T (30 ml) Rice wine, 1 T (15 ml) Salt Pepper	Snap off tough root ends of asparagus. Cut into bite-sized sections. Drain baby corn and cut into bite-sized pieces if necessary. Heat wok until very hot. Add oil. Add asparagus and stir for 1 minute. Add baby corn and stir until heated. Add wine. Season with salt and pepper.

* If the carrousel does not rotate when you place the fish on it, turn the oven tray upside down.

INGREDIENTS AND UTENSILS

PERISHABLES	PANTRY ITEMS		EQUIPMENT
whole fish 1 1/2 lb (450-680g)	rice wine	fermented black beans	wok or large skillet
asparagus 1 lb (450g)	rice	cooking oil	microwave oven
chilies	canned baby corn		
scallions	soy sauce		
fresh ginger	sesame oil		

Seafood

PRAWNS IN GARLIC SAUCE

ASPARAGUS WITH WOOD EARS

SILVER THREAD ROLLS

SERVES 3 TO 4

Wood ears are also called "tree ears". They are mushrooms growing on wood. They don't have much flavor but have a rather interesting texture. Buy the small wood ears from Sichuan; they soften in warm water in 3 minutes.

INGREDIENTS	INSTRUCTIONS
• Step 1. Silver thread rolls, 4-6*	Remove rolls from freezer and wrap in damp towel.
• Step 2. Wood ears, 1/4 C (60 ml)	Soak wood ears in warm water.
• Step 3. Water, 2 C (480 ml) Large shrimp, 1 lb (450 g) Salt, 1 t (5 ml) Scallion, 1 Ginger, 3 slices	Bring water to a boil. Meanwhile, slit back of shrimp open with a pair of kitchen shears and de-vein, but leave shells on. Rinse shrimp under cold water. Add salt, scallion and ginger to boiling water. Boil for 1 minute. Add shrimp. When water boils again, boil shrimp for 2 minutes. Remove from heat and allow to stand for another 2 minutes. Drain shrimp and arrange on serving platter.
• Step 4. Garlic, 3 cloves Ginger, 3 slices Scallion,1 Sugar, 2 t (10 ml) Soy sauce, 1 T (15 ml) Rice vinegar, 2 T (30 ml) Water, 1 T (15 ml)	Meanwhile, smash garlic and remove skin. Mince garlic and ginger. Dice scallion. Combine all ingredients listed. Pour over top of shrimp (Step 3) and serve either warm or chilled.
• Step 5.	Microwave rolls (Step 1), still wrapped in damp towel, on high for 1 to 3 minutes, or steam briefly.
• Step 6. Asparagus, 1 lb (450 g) Cooking oil, 1 T (15 ml) Sesame oil, 1 t (5 ml) Sugar, 1/2 t (3 ml) Rice vinegar, 1 t (5 ml) Salt to taste	Use a knife to peel off the tough root ends of asparagus. Cut asparagus into sections. Heat wok until very hot. As wok heats, drain water from wood ears (Step 2) and rinse off sand. Add cooking oil and sesame oil to wok. Add wood ears and stir for 10 seconds. Add asparagus, stir until cooked, about 2 minutes. Sprinkle sugar, vinegar and salt.

* If not available, use Brown 'N Serve sourdough dinner rolls.

INGREDIENTS AND EQUIPMENT

PERISHABLES	PANTRY ITEMS	EQUIPMENT
large shrimp 1 lb (450g)	cooking oil	wok or large skillet
asparagus 1 lb (450g)	sesame oil	saucepan
silver thread rolls	soy sauce	
scallion	rice vinegar	
fresh ginger	garlic	
	wood ears	

FRIED RICE WITH CARB MEAT

CARROTS WITH WALNUTS

You can make this meal in 15 minutes, provided you have enough leftover rice.

INGREDIENTS	INSTRUCTIONS
• Step 1. Sugar, 1 t (5 ml) Sesame oil, 1 t (5 ml) Rice vinegar, 1 T (15 ml) Shredded carrots, 1/2 lb (230 g), from salad bar Salt Pepper Walnuts, 2 T (30 ml)	Combine sugar, sesame oil, vinegar and carrots. Add salt and pepper to taste. Garnish with walnuts and serve.
• Step 2. Red bell pepper, 1/2 Snow peas, 20 Cooking oil, 1 T (15 ml) Sesame oil, 1 t (5 ml) Ginger, 3 slices Cooked crab meat, 1/2 lb (230 g)	Dice pepper. Nip ends of snow peas and discard strings. Heat wok until very hot. Add cooking oil and sesame oil, then add ginger, bell pepper, and snow peas. Add crab meat and stir briefly.
• Step 3. Pre-cooked rice, 3 C (720 ml), chilled Scallions, 2 Bean sprouts, 1/4 lb (110 g) Salt	Add rice to wok. Stir intermittently. Allow some of the rice to get crusty as this will enhance the flavor of the dish. Meanwhile, dice scallions. Discard ginger from wok. Add bean sprouts and stir briefly. Sprinkle a dash of salt to season. Garnish with scallions.

INGREDIENTS AND EQUIPMENT

PERISHABLES
cooked crab meat 1/2 lb (230g)
shredded carrots 1/2 lb (230g)
red bell pepper 1/2
snow peas 20
bean sprouts 1/4 lb (110g)
fresh ginger
scallions
pre-cooked rice

PANTRY ITEMS
cooking oil
sesame oil
rice vinegar
walnuts

EQUIPMENT
wok or large skillet

CANTONESE LOBSTER

ASPARAGUS IN OYSTER DRESSING

RICE

Include these dishes in your next banquet! Your guests will think that it took you hours to make a dinner like this. Read the recipe carefully before you start.

INGREDIENTS

INSTRUCTIONS

• Step 1. Asparagus, 1 lb (450 g)

Snap off tough root ends of asparagus. Arrange asparagus on platter. Sprinkle with 1 T (15 ml) of water, cover and microwave on high until tender, about 6 minutes, rotating midway. When asparagus is cooked, plunge into cold water to cool. Drain.

• Step 2. Rice, 1 C (240 ml)
Water, 2 C (480 ml)

Meanwhile, wash rice. Place with water in rangetop casserole. Bring to boil over high heat. Boil uncovered for 1 minute. Turn heat to the lowest setting. Cover and simmer from 5 to 10 minutes. Keep covered until dinner time. Don't stir. As the rice cooks, do the following:

• Step 3. Sugar, 1 t (5 ml)
Oyster sauce, 1 T (15 ml)
Soy sauce, 1 T (15 ml)
Sesame oil, 1 t (5 ml)
Water, 1 T (15 ml)

Mix all ingredients listed and set aside. Arrange asparagus (Step 1) neatly on the platter in one direction. Cut across the stems into small setions. Pour the mixture over the asparagus when you are ready to serve.

• Step 4. Garlic, 3 cloves
Ginger, 3 slices
Fermented black beans,
   1 T (15 ml)
Cooking oil, 2 T (30 ml)
Ground pork, 1/4 lb (110 g)
Lobster, steamed and sectioned,
   1 1/2 lb (680 g)
Rice wine, 1 t (5 ml)
Thin soy sauce, 1 T (15 ml)
Sugar, 1/2 t (3 ml)
Chicken broth, canned,
   1 C (240 ml)

Remove skin from garlic cloves. Mince garlic, ginger and black beans. Heat wok until very hot. Add oil. Add garlic, ginger and black beans, stir for 10 seconds. Add pork and stir until color changes. Add lobster, stir for 1 minute. Splash in wine. Add soy sauce and sugar. Stir once. Add broth and bring to a boil. Reduce heat, cover and simmer for 3 minutes.

• Step 5. Egg, 1
Scallion, 1
Cornstarch, 1 T (15 ml)
Water, 1 T (15 ml)

Meanwhile, beat egg and dice scallion. Mix cornstarch with water to make paste. Stir paste slowly into the lobster in Step 4. Stop adding paste when sauce is thick enough. Add egg to wok and stir. Transfer to serving platter. Garnish with scallion.

INGREDIENTS AND EQUIPMENT

PERISHABLES	PANTRY ITEMS		EQUIPMENT
live lobster 1 (ask the fish person to steam and chop into bite-size pieces)	cornstarch	canned chicken broth	wok or large skillet
ground pork 1/4 lb (110g)	cooking oil	rice	with cover
asparagus 1 lb (450g)	sesame oil	rice wine	microwave oven
fresh ginger	thin soy sauce		
eggs	oyster sauce		
scallion	garlic		
	fermented black beans		

SHRIMP AND BROCCOLI IN BLACK BEAN SAUCE

RICE

SERVES 2 TO 3

You may be tempted to buy ready-shelled shrimp to save time. But I have found that they are never as flavorful as the ones you shell yourself. If you must save time, buy the large shrimp or use scallops instead.

INGREDIENTS	INSTRUCTIONS
• Step 1. Large shrimp, 3/4 lb (340 g) Salt, 1/4 t (1 ml) Cornstarch, 1 t (5 ml) Rice wine, 1 t (5 ml)	Shell and de-vein shrimp. Split lengthwise if large. Mix with remaining ingredients listed.
• Step 2. Rice, 3/4 C (180 ml) Water, 1 1/2 C (360 ml)	Wash rice. Place with water in a rangetop casserole. Bring to boil over high heat. Boil uncovered for 1 minute. Turn heat to the lowest setting. Cover and simmer anywhere from 5 to 15 minutes. Keep covered until dinner time. Don't stir. As the rice cooks, do the following:
• Step 3. Broccoli florets, 1/4 lb (110 g)	Cut broccoli florets into bite-sized pieces. Arrange on microwave platter. Sprinkle with 1 T (15 ml) water. Cover and microwave for 1 minute. Plunge into cold water to cool. Drain.
• Step 4. Garlic, 3 cloves Ginger, 3 slices Fermented black beans, 1 T (15 ml) Hot bean paste, 1 t (5 ml), optional	Smash garlic to loosen skin. Remove skin. Mince ginger and garlic. Combine all ingredients listed.
• Step 5. Scallion, 1 Cooking oil, 2 T (30 ml) Sliced water chestnuts, 1 C (240 ml) Soy sauce to taste	Heat wok until very hot. As wok heats, dice scallion. Swirl oil into wok. Add mixture prepared in Step 4, stir for 10 seconds. Add shrimp (Step 1) and stir until no more translucent. Add broccoli (Step 3) and water chestnuts, stir briefly. Add scallion. Sprinkle soy sauce and serve.

INGREDIENTS AND EQUIPMENT

PERISHABLES	PANTRY ITEMS		EQUIPMENT
large shrimp 3/4 lb (340g)	cornstarch	garlic	wok or large skillet
broccoli florets 1/4 lb (110g)	rice wine	fermented black beans	microwave oven
fresh ginger	cooking oil	hot bean paste	rangetop casserole
scallions	rice	sliced water chestnuts	
	soy sauce		

NOODLES WITH SHRIMP AND PORK

SERVES 2 TO 3

Try fresh Chinese noodles. They boil fast, often less than a minute, yet delicious to eat. You find them in freezers or refrigerators at Chinese grocery stores. Frozen ones can be boiled without being thawed first. Use either the narrow ones or wide ones. They can be either made with eggs (yellow) or without (ivory).

INGREDIENTS	INSTRUCTIONS
• Step 1.	Place 3 quarts (3 liters) water in a large pot, cover and bring to a boil.
• Step 2. Shrimp, 1/2 lb (230 g) Pork 1/4 lb (110 g) Salt, 1/4 t (1 ml) Pepper, 1/4 t (1 ml) Cornstarch, 1 t (5 ml) Rice wine, 1 t (5 ml) Soy sauce, 1 T (15 ml)	Meanwhile, shell and de-vein shrimp. Slice pork thinly. Mix shrimp and pork with remaining ingredients and set aside.
• Step 3. Snow peas, 1/4 lb (110 g)	Nip ends of snow peas and remove strings. Place on plate, sprinkle with a little water, cover and microwave on high for 1 minute, or blanch briefly in boiling water. Plunge into cold water to cool. Drain.
• Step 4. Fresh Chinese noodles, 1 lb (450 g) Sesame oil, 1 t (5 m)	Add noodles to boiling water prepared in Step 1. Boil noodles until *al dente*. This should take less than 1 minute. Drain and rinse with cold water until cool. Mix with sesame oil.
• Step 5. Scallions, 2	Dice scallions.
• Step 6. Black mushrooms, canned, 6 Cooking oil, 2 T (30 ml) Bean sprouts, 1/4 lb (110 g)	Heat wok until very hot. While wok heats, slice mushrooms. Add oil to heated wok. Add shrimp and pork (Step 2), stir until color changes. Add mushrooms and snow peas (Step 3), stir briefly. Add noodles (Step 4), stir until heated. Add bean sprouts, stir for 2 minutes. Don't overcook. Transfer to serving platter. Garnish with scallions (Step 5).
• Step 7. Soy sauce Chili oil Rice vinegar	Use the ingredients listed as condiments.

INGREDIENTS AND EQUIPMENT

PERISHABLES	PANTRY ITEMS		EQUIPMENT
large shrimp 1/2 lb (230g)	cornstarch	rice vinegar	wok
pork 1/4 lb (110g)	rice wine	canned black mushrooms	large saucepan
snow peas 1/4 lb (110g)	soy sauce		microwave oven
bean sprouts 1/4 lb (110g)	cooking oil		
fresh Chinese noodles 1 lb (450g)	sesame oil		
scallions	chili oil		

BRAISED SHRIMP

GREEN BEANS WITH TIANJIN VEGETBABLE

RICE

SERVES 3 TO 4

This shrimp dish is easy to make. It can be used either as a main dish or an appetizer. If you want to make this dish only, just follow the text printed on   .

INGREDIENTS	INSTRUCTIONS
• Step 1. Rice, 1 C (240 ml) Water, 2 C (480 ml)	Wash rice. Place with water in a rangetop casserole. Bring to boil over high heat. Boil uncovered for 1 minute. Turn heat to the lowest setting, cover and simmer anywhere between 5 to 10 minutes. Let stay covered until dinner is served. Don't stir.
• Step 2. Large shrimp, 1 lb (450 g)	Using a pair of kitchen shears or a serrated knife, slit open the back of shrimp to de-vein. Don't remove shells. Rinse under cold water. Blot dry with paper towel.
• Step 3. Garlic, 3 cloves Cooking oil, 2 T (30 ml) Ginger, 3 slices Salt, 1/2 t (3 ml)	Heat skillet over medium heat. Smash garlic to loosen skin. Remove skin. Add oil to skillet. Fry garlic and ginger until fragrant. Discard both. Reduce heat. Brown one side of shrimp (Step 2) by cooking in flavored oil. Sprinkle one-half of salt. Turn shrimp over and repeat.
• Step 4. Sugar, 2 t (10 ml) Rice vinegar, 2 t (10 ml) Rice wine, 1 T (15 ml) Soy sauce, 1 T (15 ml) Ketchup, 1/4 C (60 ml) Water, 3 T (45 ml)	Combine all ingredients listed. Sprinkle on shrimp (Step 3). Cover and simmer until shrimp is completely cooked (it should turn pink). Arrange shrimp on serving platter. Pour sauce from skillet over shrimp.
• Step 5. Tianjin vegetable, 1/4 C (60 ml) Cooking oil, 1 T (15 ml) Sesame oil, 1 t (5 ml) Frozen green beans, 1 lb (450 g) Water, 1/3 C (80 ml) Rice vinegar, 1 t (5 ml)	Heat wok until hot. As wok heats, rinse Tianjin vegetable. Add cooking oil and sesame oil. Add Tianjin vegetable and stir briefly. Add green beans and stir until completely thawed. Add water, cover and cook over high heat for 3 minutes. Open and stir until beans are tender and most of the moisture has been absorbed. Stir in vinegar and serve.

INGREDIENTS AND EQUIPMENT

PERISHABLES	PANTRY ITEMS		EQUIPMENT
large shrimp 1 lb (450g) frozen green beans 1 lb (450g) fresh ginger	rice vinegar rice wine cooking oil sesame oil garlic	long grain rice ketchup soy sauce Tianjin vegetable	skillet with cover wok with cover

CRAB MEAT FU YUNG

PRESSED TOFU AND CELERY SALAD

STEAMED BUNS

SERVES 3 TO 4

Buy steamed buns from Chinese store—refrigerators or freezers. Make sure you don't overheat them in the microwave oven—they would become chewy. If you can't find steamed buns, use Brown 'N Serve sourdough dinner rolls. Heat them wrapped in a damp kitchen towel the same way you would steamed buns. They taste very Chinese that way.

INGREDIENTS	INSTRUCTIONS
• Step 1. Steamed buns, 6	Remove buns from freezer and wrap in damp towel.
• Step 2. Celery stalks, 5 or 2 C (480 ml) ready-sliced Brown pressed tofu, 1/2 lb (230 g) Sugar, 1 t (5 ml) Rice vinegar, 2 t (10 ml) Sesame oil, 2 t (10 ml) Soy sauce to taste	Slice celery thin. Place on microwave-safe plate, sprinkle with 1 T (15 ml) water, cover and microwave on high for 2 minutes. Plunge into cold water to cool. Drain. Meanwhile, julienne-cut tofu. Mix celery and tofu with remaining ingredients listed. Serve chilled or at room temperature.
• Step 3. Scallion, 1	Dice scallion.
• Step 4. Eggs, 6 Salt, a dash Cooking oil, 2 T (30 ml) Sesame oil, 1 t (5 ml) Ginger, 3 slices Cooked crab meat, 1/2 lb (230 g) Bean sprouts, 2 C (480 ml) White pepper, a dash	Heat skillet until hot. While skillet is heating, beat eggs together with salt. Pour 1 T of cooking oil and sesame oil into heated skillet. Add ginger and stir briefly. Add crab meat and stir until heated. Add scallion, bean sprouts and pepper, stir briefly. Discard ginger. Remove mixture to a bowl temporarily. Wash out skillet and return to stovetop over medium heat. Add 1 T of cooking oil. Pour in eggs. Swirl skillet to spread eggs. Spread crab meat mixture over top of eggs. When eggs are partially set, cut with a spatula into sections and turn over each section to cook the other side. Cook until eggs are completely set.
• Step 5.	Microwave buns wrapped in towel for 1 to 3 minutes on high.

INGREDIENTS AND EQUIPMENT

PERISHABLES		PANTRY ITEMS	EQUIPMENT
cooked crab meat 1/2 lb (230g)	steamed buns	rice vinegar	large skillet
brown pressed tofu 1/2 lb (230g)	celery	cooking oil	microwave oven
eggs	bean sprouts 2 C	sesame oil	
ginger		soy sauce	
scallions		white pepper	

NOODLES WITH CARB MEAT AND EGGS

SERVES 2 TO 3

Fresh snow peas add color, taste, and crunchiness to the dishes you cook. Frozen snow peas are no substitute. If you substitute frozen green peas for fresh snow peas, they will at least add some bright green color and sweet taste.

INGREDIENTS	INSTRUCTIONS
• Step 1.	Bring large pot of water to a boil.
• Step 2. Cooked crab meat, 1/2 lb (230 g) Salt, 1/4 t (1 ml) White pepper, a dash Rice wine, 1 t (5 ml)	Mix all ingredients listed.
• Step 3. Snow peas, 1/4 lb (110 g)	Pinch ends of snow peas, remove strings.
• Step 4. Chicken broth, two 14 oz (400 g) cans Water, 2 C (480 ml)	In a small pot, combine broth and water and bring to a boil.
• Step 5. Eggs, 3 Cooking oil, 1 T (15 ml)	Heat large skillet over medium heat. As it heats, beat the eggs. Add oil to skillet, swirl to spread evenly. Reduce heat and add eggs. Swirl skillet again to spread eggs in a thin layer. Fry eggs to make an egg pancake. When fully cooked, transfer pancake to a cutting board and slice it into long strips.
• Step 6. Dried Chinese noodles, 1/2 lb (230 g) Sesame oil, 2 t (10 ml) Scallion, 1	Add noodles to pot of boiling water prepared in Step 1. Cook until *al dente*, about 1 to 2 minutes. Drain and mix with sesame oil to prevent from sticking together. Place in soup tureen. Dice scallions and set aside.
• Step 7. Black mushrooms, one 10 oz (280 g) can Water chestnuts, sliced, 1 cup Rice vinegar, a dash	Drain mushrooms and water chestnuts. Add them to boiling broth prepared in Step 4. Add egg strips (Step 5). Wait for broth to return to a boil, then add snow peas (Step 3). Let them boil briefly. Pour content of pot over noodles (Step 6). Garnish with crab meat (Step 2) and scallion (Step 6). Add a dash of vinegar and serve.

INGREDIENTS AND EQUIPMENT

PERISHABLES	PANTRY ITEMS		EQUIPMENT
cooked crab meat 1/2 lb (230g)	white pepper	Chinese noodles, thin and dried	large skillet
snow peas 1/4 lb (110g)	rice wine	canned chicken broth	large pot
scallions	cooking oil	sliced water chestnuts	small pot
eggs	rice vinegar	canned black mushrooms	
	sesame oil		

CAULIFLOWER AND CRAB MEAT

PRESSED TOFU AND PEPPERS

RICE WITH SESAME SEEDS

SERVES 3 TO 4

I can't recommend tofu enough to you. High in protein, low in saturated fat, and low in price, too. But the texture and blandness tend to turn away most beginners. Why not start with the pressed tofu? It is firmer and absorbs spices more readily, making it much more flavorful.

INGREDIENTS	INSTRUCTIONS
• Step 1. Cooked crab meat, 1/2 lb (230 g) Salt, 1/4 t (1 ml) White pepper, a dash Rice wine, 1 t (5 ml)	Mix all ingredients listed together.
• Step 2. Rice, 1 C (240 ml) Water, 2 C (480 ml) Black sesame seeds, 1 T (15 ml)	Wash rice. Place with water in a rangetop casserloe. Bring to boil over high heat. Boil for 1 minute, uncovered. Turn heat to the lowest setting, cover and simmer for 5 to 10 minutes. Keep covered until dinner time. Don't stir. Garnish with sesame seeds before serving. While the rice cooks, do the following:
• Step 3. Brown pressed tofu, 1 lb (450 g) Bell peppers, 2 Sugar, 2 t (10 ml) Sesame oil, 1 t (5 ml) Rice vinegar, 1 T (15 ml) Chili oil, 1 t (5 ml)	Cut tofu and peppers into thin strips. Mix with remaining ingredients. Add salt only if needed. Serve chilled or at room temperature.
• Step 4. Chicken broth, one 15 oz (430 g) can Cauliflower florets, 1 lb (450 g) Ginger, 3 slices Sesame oil, 1 t (5 ml) Cornstanch, 2 T (30 ml) Water, 2 T (30 ml)	In saucepan, bring broth to a boil. Meanwhile, cut cauliflower into bite-sized pieces. When broth is at a boil, add cauliflower and ginger. Cover and simmer until tender. Leaving the liquid in the saucepan, transfer cauliflower to a serving platter. Add crab meat (Step 1) and sesame oil to saucepan. Bring broth to a boil a second time. Mix cornstarch with water to make a paste. Slowly add the paste to the boiling broth until the sauce is thick enough. Discard the remaining past. Also discard ginger. Pour sauce over cauliflower and serve.

INGREDIENTS AND EQUIPMENT

PERISHABLES	PANTRY ITEMS		EQUIPMENT
cooked crab meat 1/2 lb (230g)	cornstarch	chili oil	saucepan
brown pressed tofu 1 lb (450g)	white pepper	cooking oil	rangetop casserole
cauliflower 1 lb (450g)	rice wine	canned chicken broth	
bell peppers 2, any color	sesame oil	long grain rice	
ginger	rice vinegar	black sesame seads	

SCALLOPS AND ASPARAGUS WITH BLACK BEANS

BABY CORN AND BLACK MUSHROOMS

STEAMED BUNS

SERVES 2 TO 3

Steamed buns are made of yeast dough, sugar and oil. Since you can't possibly make them in 30 minutes, buy ready-made from Chinese stores (in freezers or refrigerators). If not available, use Brown 'N Serve sourdough dinner rolls.

INGREDIENTS	INSTRUCTIONS
• Step 1. Steamed buns, 4	Remove steamed buns from freezer and wrap in damp towel.
• Step 2. Scallops, 3/4 lb (340 g) Salt, 1/2 t (3 ml) Cornstarch, 1 t (5 ml) Rice wine, 1 t (5 ml)	Cut scallops into slices. Combine with remaining ingredients listed.
• Step 3. Asparagus, 1 lb (450 g)	Snap off tough root ends of asparagus. Cut asparagus into sections. Arrange on a microwave-safe platter, with thicker pieces toward the edge. Sprinkle with 1 T (15 ml) of water, cover and microwave on high for 1 to 2 minutes. Rotate and repeat. Once cooked, place the asparagus on a different plate to cool.
• Step 4. Baby corn, one 8 oz (230 g) can Black mushrooms, one 10 oz (280 g) can Sugar, 1 t (5 ml) Oyster sauce, 1 T (15 ml) Sesame oil, 1 t (5 ml)	Drain baby corn and mushrooms. Combine sugar, oyster sauce and sesame oil. Pour over corn and mushrooms. Serve chilled or at room temperature.
• Step 5.	Microwave steamed buns (Step 1) on high without removing towel for 1 to 3 minutes.
• Step 6. Garlic, 3 cloves Ginger, 3 slices Fermented black beans, 1 T (15 ml) Scallion, 1	Smash garlic to loosen skin. Remove skin. Mince garlic, ginger and black beans. Dice scallion. Combine all ingredients.
• Step 7. Cooking oil, 2 T (30 ml) Rice wine, 1 t (5 ml)	Heat wok until very hot. Add oil. Add mixture prepared in Step 6 and stir for 10 seconds. Add scallops (Step 2) and stir until they are opaque. Add asparagus (Step 3), stir until heated. Splash in wine, stir briefly and serve.

INGREDIENTS AND EQUIPMENT

PERISHABLES	PANTRY ITEMS		EQUIPMENT
scallops 3/4 lb (340g) asparagus 1 lb (450g) steamed buns scallion fresh ginger	cornstarch rice wine cooking oil oyster sauce sesame oil	canned baby corn canned black mushrooms fermented black beans garlic	wok or large skillet microwave oven

Vegetarian

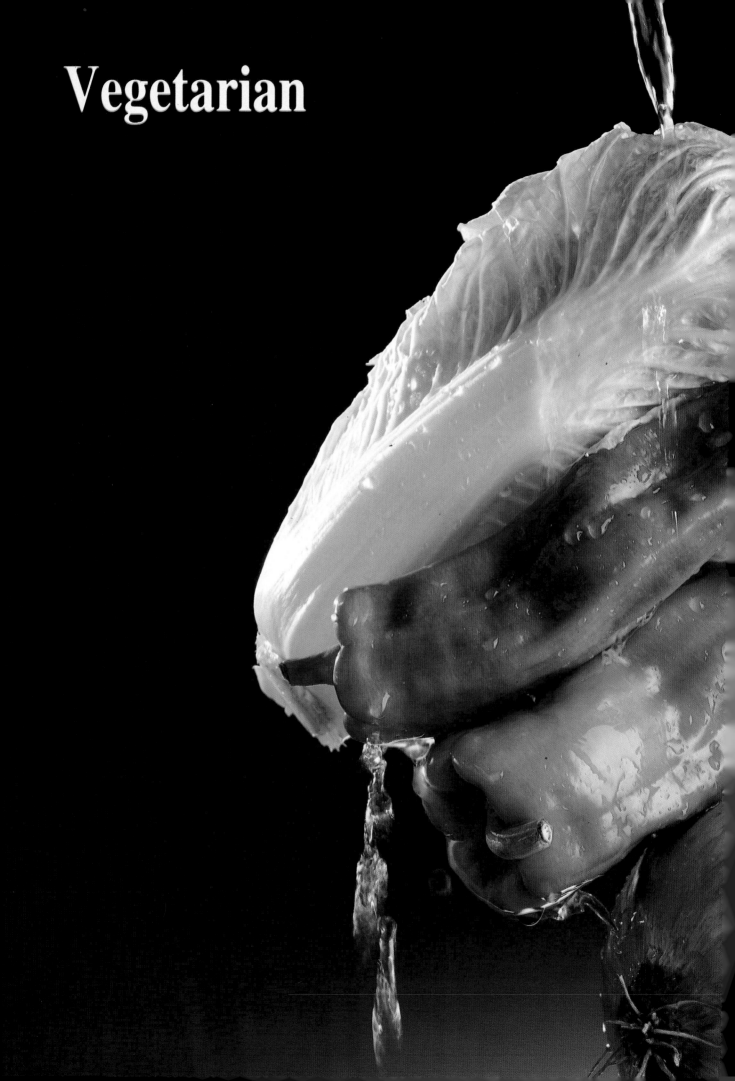

VEGETARIAN BEAN SAUCE NOODLES

This all-vegetarian dish, with brown pressed tofu and peanuts, is so satisfying that you won't miss the meat at all.

INGREDIENTS	INSTRUCTIONS
• Step 1.	Bring 3 quarts (3 liters) water to boil in a large pot.
• Step 2. Garlic, 3 cloves Ginger, 2 slices Hot bean paste, 2 t (10 ml) Hoisin sauce, 1 T (15 ml)	Smash garlic to loosen skin. Remove skin. Mince garlic and ginger. Combine all ingredients listed.
• Step 3. Brown pressed tofu, 1/2 lb (230 g) Cooking oil, 1 T (15 ml) Sesame oil, 1 t (5 ml) Frozen mixed vegetables, 10 oz (280 g) Peanuts, 1/4 C (60 ml) Sugar, 1 t (5 ml) Dark soy sauce, 1 T (15 ml) Water, 1 C (240 ml) Cornstarch, 2 t (10 ml) Water, 1 T (15 ml)	Dice pressed tofu. Heat wok until very hot. Swirl in cooking oil and sesame oil. Add ingredients prepared in Step 2 and stir for 10 seconds. Add tofu, stir for 1 minute. Add mixed vegetables, stir for 2 minutes. Add peanuts, sugar and soy sauce, stir briefly. Add water and bring to a boil. Cover and steam over medium heat for 2 minutes. Meanwhile, mix cornstarch and water to make paste. Remove cover and stir in paste slowly to thicken the mixture. Set aside for later use.
• Step 4. Fresh Chinese noodles, 1 lb (450 g) Bean sprouts, 1/2 lb (230 g) Sesame oil, 1 t (5 ml)	Add noodles to pot of boiling water prepared in Step 1. Boil until cooked but still firm, about 1 minute. Add bean sprouts, then quickly drain sprouts and noodles together using a colander. Mix with sesame oil to prevent from sticking together. Transfer to a serving platter. Pour mixture from Step 3 over the top and serve.
• Step 5. Sesame paste, 2 T (30 ml) Scallions diced, 2 Rice vinegar Soy sauce Chili oil	Use these items as condiments. Mix together and add to your noodles or let each person add separately to his or her noodles. Before using the sesame paste, add 1/4 cup (60 ml) water to it slowly, stir it at the same time to make a smooth paste.

INGREDIENTS AND EQUIPMENT

PERISHABLES	PANTRY ITEMS		EQUIPMENT
brown pressed tofu 1/2 lb (230g)	cornstarch	chili oil	wok or large skillet
frozen mixed vegetables 10 oz (280g)	cooking oil	hot bean paste	large kettle
fresh ginger	dark soy sauce	hoisin sauce	colander
scallion	rice vinegar	peanuts, roasted or raw	
fresh Chinese noodles	sesame paste	garlic	
bean sprouts 1/2 lb (230g)	sesame oil		

EGGS AND TOMATOES

SICHUAN MA LAH TOFU

RICE

"Ma Lah" is a unique Sichuan flavor which is hard to explain to the uninitiated. "Ma" is the numbing sensation created by Sichuan pepper, "Lah" is the hot sensation created by chili oil. Put the two together and you have a dynamite combination! You can either buy the ground Sichuan pepper in a spice bottle or crush the peppercorn yourself with the cleaver handle or grind it in a pepper mill.

INGREDIENTS	INSTRUCTIONS
• Step 1. Tofu, 1 lb (450 g)	Remove tofu from package and place on plate to drain.
• Step 2. Rice, 3/4 C (180 ml) Water, 1 1/2 C (360 ml)	Wash rice. Place with water in a rangetop casserole. Bring to boil over high heat. Boil for 1 minute, uncovered. Turn heat to the lowest setting, cover and simmer for 5 to 10 minutes. Keep covered until dinner time. Don't stir. While the rice cooks, do the following:
• Step 3. Garlic, 3 cloves Ground Sichuan pepper, 1/4 t (1 ml) Chili oil, 2 t (10 ml) Sugar, 2 t (10 ml) Rice vinegar, 2 t (10 ml) Soy sauce, 1 T (15 ml) Sesame oil, 1 t (5 ml) Cilantro, a few sprigs	Smash garlic to loosen and remove skin. Mix all ingredients listed with the exception of cilantro. Discard excess moisture from tofu (Step 1) and pour mixture over. Garnish with cilantro. Serve chilled or at room temperature.
• Step 4. Tomatoes, 2 Eggs, 6 Salt, a dash Scallion, 1 Cooking oil, 3 T (45 ml) Sesame oil, 1 t (5 ml) Oyster sauce, 1 T (15 ml)	Cut tomatoes into wedges. Discard juice and seeds. Beat eggs together with salt. Heat skillet until very hot. While skillet heats, dice scallion. Add 1 T (15 ml) of cooking oil to skillet. Add tomato wedges and stir for 1 minute. Set tomatoes aside. Rinse out skillet. Heat it until very hot again, then add remaining 2 T (30 ml) of cooking oil and sesame oil. Add eggs, reduce heat. Cook eggs until they are partially set, then spread tomato wedges over the top of eggs. When eggs are almost cooked, turn over, a spatulaful at a time, to cook completely. Sprinkle oyster sauce on top and garnish with diced scallion.

INGREDIENTS AND EQUIPMENT

PERISHABLES	PANTRY ITEMS		EQUIPMENT
tofu 1 lb (450 lb) soft	garlic	osyter sauce	skillet
tomatoes 2	ground Sichuan pepper	rice vinegar	
scallions	cooking oil	rice	
eggs	sesame oil	soy sauce	
cilantro	chili oil		

BUDDHA'S FEAST

SCALLIONS ROLLS

Strict Buddhists are pure vegetarians. To accommodate any lingering hankering after meat, Buddhists use tofu and wheat products to create astonishingly look-and taste-alikes of meat, poultry and seafood. See "WHEAT GLUTEN" on page 156.

INGREDIENTS	INSTRUCTIONS
• Step 1. Scallion rolls, 4	Remove scallion rolls from freezer and wrap in damp towel.

• Step 2. Golden needles, 1/4 C (60 ml)
Wood ears, 1/4 C (60 ml)
Bean threads, one 2 oz
    (60 g) bundle
Carrot, 1
Cauliflower florets,
    1 C (240 ml)
Broccoli florets, 1 C (240 ml)
	Soak golden needles and wood ears together in warm water. Soak bean threads in warm water separately. Peel and slice carrot. Cut cauliflower and broccoli in bite-sized pieces.

• Step 3. Wheat gluten, one 10 oz
    (280 g) jar
Black mushrooms, one
    10 oz (280 g) can
	Drain golden needles and wood ears when soft (Step 2). Rinse off sand. Drain bean threads (Step 2) and cut across a few times. Drain gluten and mushrooms.

• Step 4. Cooking oil, 1 T (15 ml) Sesame oil, 1 t (5 ml) Sugar, 1 t (5 ml) Soy sauce, 1 t (5 ml) Water, 1/4 C (60 ml) Walnuts, 2 T (30 ml)	Heat wok until very hot. Swirl in cooking oil and sesame oil. Add golden needles and wood ears (Step 3) and stir for 30 seconds. Add items in following order, stir until heated each time: carrot, cauliflower, broccoli (Step 2), gluten, mushrooms (Step 3). Add sugar and soy sauce, then water. Add bean threads (Step 3), stir until items are fully cooked, about 2 minutes. Garnish with walnuts and serve.
• Step 5.	Microwave scallion rolls (Step 1), still wrapped in damp towel, on high for 1 to 3 minutes.

INGREDIENTS AND EQUIPMENT

PERISHABLES	PANTRY ITEMS		EQUIPMENT
scallion rolls	golden needles	cooking oil	wok or large skillet
carrot	wood ears	sesame oil	microwave oven
cauliflower florets 1 cup (240ml)	bean threads	soy sauce	
broccoli florets 1 cup (240ml)	wheat gluten	walnuts	
	canned black mushrooms		

TOFU IN CRAB MEAT SAUCE

FOUR-JEWELLED VEGETABLES

RICE

SERVES 2 TO 3

To make this a strict vegetarian meal, substitute crab meat with Sichuan vegetable and chicken broth with vegetable broth. The dish will have a different color, taste and texture, but it will still be delicious.

INGREDIENTS	INSTRUCTIONS
• Step 1. Tofu, 1 lb (450 g)	Remove tofu from package and place on plate to drain.
• Step 2. Rice, 3/4 C (180 ml) Water, 1 1/2 C (360 ml)	Wash rice. Place with water in a rangetop casserole. Bring to boil over high heat. Boil uncovered for 1 minute. Turn heat to the lowest setting, cover and simmer anywhere between 5 to 10 minutes. Let stay covered until dinner is served. Don't stir.
• Step 3. Snow peas, 6 oz (170 g) Sliced water chestnuts, one 6 oz (170 g) can Black mushrooms, two 10 oz (280 g) cans Golden needle mushrooms, two 8 oz (230 g) cans	Nip ends of snow peas and remove strings. Drain water chestnuts, black mushrooms and golden needle mushrooms.
• Step 4. Chicken broth, canned, 1 C (240 ml) Sugar, 1/2 t (3 ml) White pepper, a dash Ginger, 3 slices Oyster sauce, 1 T (15 ml)	Bring broth to a boil in a skillet. Add sugar, pepper, ginger and oyster sauce. Stir. Let boil for 1 minute. Carefully slice tofu (Step 1) into 3/4 inch (2 cm) thick pieces. Lower tofu pieces into skillet gently. Allow broth to boil again, then reduce heat, cover and simmer for 3 minutes. Next, using two spatulas, turn tofu pieces over and simmer another 2 minutes with the lid on. Discard ginger. Remove tofu to a serving platter and keep warm.
• Step 5. Cooked crab meat, 1/4 lb (110 g) Cornstarch, 1 T (15 ml) Water, 1 T (15 ml) Cilantro, a sprig	Add crab meat to liquid remaining in skillet (Step 4). Bring liquid to a boil. Mix cornstarch and water to make a paste. Slowly add paste to the boiling broth to thicken it. Pour mixture over tofu (Step 4). Garnish with cilantro.
• Step 6. Garlic, 3 cloves Cooking oil, 2 T (30 ml) Sugar, 1/2 t (3 ml) Salt, a dash Pepper, a dash	Heat wok until very hot. Meanwhile, remove skin from garlic cloves. Add oil to heated wok. Add garlic. Add snow peas (Step 3), stir for 1 minute. Add water chestnuts, mushrooms and golden needle mushrooms (Step 3), one by one and stir each until heated. Sprinkle sugar, salt and pepper. Discard garlic and serve.

INGREDIENTS AND EQUIPMENT

PERISHABLES	PANTRY ITEMS		EQUIPMENT
tofu 1 lb (450g) snow peas 6 oz (170g) fresh ginger cooked crab meat 1/4 lb (110g) cilantro	canned water chestnuts canned black mushrooms canned golden needle mushrooms canned chicken broth	white pepper oyster sauce cornstarch garlic cooking oil rice	skillet with cover wok

EGGS AND SCALLIONS

PRESSED TOFU AND CUCUMBERS

SPRING ROLL WRAPPERS

SERVES 3 TO 4

Enchanted by the beauty of Chinese characters, an American lady copied the sign she saw in a Chinese restaurant and embroidered it on her beautiful silk dress. She wore it proudly on a date with a Chinese man. "You like this?" she asked, "What does this say?" He replied: "This dish is nutritious, delicious and cheap".

INGREDIENTS

INSTRUCTIONS

• Step 1.
Pickling cucumbers,
  1/2 lb (230 g)
Brown pressed tofu,
  1/2 lb (230 g)
Red chili, 1
Garlic, 3 cloves
Sugar, 1 t (5 ml)
Soy sauce, 1 T (15 ml), or to taste
Sesame oil, 1 t (5 ml)
Rice vinegar, 2 t (10 ml)

Wash cucumbers, but don't remove skin. Julienne-cut cucumbers and tofu. Open chili and wash away seeds. Cut into thin strips. Remove skin from garlic, mince garlic. Mix all ingredients. Serve chilled or at room temperature.

• Step 2.
Scallions, 3
Eggs, 6
Salt, a dash
Cooking oil, 2 T (30 ml)
Sesame oil, 1 t (5 ml)
Oyster sauce, 1 T (15 ml)

Dice scallions. Heat wok until very hot. As wok heats, beat eggs together with salt and scallions. Add cooking oil and sesame oil to wok. Stir in eggs and reduce heat. When eggs are almost set, turn them over, a spatulaful at a time, until completely cooked. Transfer to serving platter. Garnish with oyster sauce.

• Step 3.
Shanghai spring roll
  wrappers, 15-20

Wrap wrappers in damp towel and microwave on high for 20 to 40 seconds, or longer if frozen. (Or steam briefly). Roll tofu and cucumbers (Step 1) and eggs (Step 2) in wrappers to eat.

INGREDIENTS AND EQUIPMENT

PERISHABLES	PANTRY ITEMS	EQUIPMENT
pickling cucumbers 1/2 lb (230g)	garlic	wok or skillet
brown pressed tofu 1/2 lb (230g)	sesame oil	
red chilies	rice vinegar	
Shanghai spring roll wrappers	cooking oil	
scallions	oyster sauce	
eggs	soy sauce	

FISH-FRAGRANT EGGPLANT

TOFU WITH PEANUTS

RICE

SERVES 2 TO 3

Something is "fishy" about an eggplant being called "fish-fragrant." Eggplant doesn't look like fish; it doesn't taste like fish; fish is not even used as an ingredient. Then why is it called "fish-fragrant?" Perhaps a fish dish was made long ago with similar spices; or more likely, "fish-fragrant" suggested culinary sophistication. In any case, it is not at all fishy to say that the dish tastes great. Enjoy it!

INGREDIENTS	INSTRUCTIONS
• Step 1. Tofu, soft, 1 lb (450 g)	Remove tofu from package, place on plate to drain.
• Step 2. Rice, 3/4 C (180 ml) Water, 1 1/2 C (360 ml)	Wash rice. Place with water in a rangetop casserole. Bring to boil over high heat. Boil uncovered for 1 minute. Turn heat to the lowest setting, cover and simmer for 5 to 10 minutes. Let stay covered until dinner is served. Don't stir.
• Step 3. Garlic cloves, 3 Ginger, 3 slices Hot bean paste, 1 t (5 ml), or to taste Eggplant, 1 lb (450 g)	Smash garlic to loosen and remove skin. Mince garlic and ginger. Combine with hot bean paste. If Oriental eggplants are used, don't peel, just slice diagonally. If a regular eggplant is used, peel and quarter eggplant, cut into thin slices.
• Step 4. Salt, 1/4 t (1 ml) Sugar, 1/2 t (3 ml) Rice vinegar, 2 t (10 ml) Sesame oil, 1 t (5 ml) Soy sauce, 1 T (15 ml)	Combine all ingredients listed.
• Step 5. Cooking oil, 3 T (45 ml) Ground pork or chicken, 1/4 lb (110 g) Water, 1/4 C (60 ml) Scallion, 1	Heat wok until very hot. Add oil. Add garlic, ginger and hot bean paste combination (Step 3) and stir for 10 seconds. Add ground pork or chicken, stir until almost cooked. Add eggplant (Step 3) and stir. Add mixture prepared in Step 4. Stir briefly. Add water, stir intermittently until most liquid evaportes and the eggplant had turned dark. Meanwhile, dice scallion. When eggplant is ready, garnish with scallions.
• Step 6. Salt, 1/4 t (1 ml) Sugar, 1 t (5 ml) Rice vinegar, 2 t (10 ml) Soy sauce 1 T (15 ml) Sesame oil, 1 t (5 ml) Roasted peanuts, 2 T (30 ml)	Drain liquid further from tofu (Step 1), mix all ingredients listed except for peanuts. Pour mixture over tofu. Garnish with peanuts.

INGREDIENTS AND EQUIPMENT

PERISHABLES	PANTRY ITEMS		EQUIPMENT
ground meat or chicken 1/4 lb (110g)	cooking oil	hot bean paste	wok or large skillet
eggplant (s) 1 lb (450g)	rice vinegar	roasted peanuts	small stovetop casserole
soft tofu 1 lb (450g)	long grain rice	garlic	
ginger	soy sauce		
scallion	sesame oil		

SWEET AND SOUR CUCUMERS

SERVES 2 TO 3

If you ever have 3 or more cups of leftover rice, make egg-fried rice. Make it colorful as my mother did. Don't try to imitate the restaurant version with everything brown, yuk!

INGREDIENTS

- Step 1. Pickling cucumbers, 1 lb (450 g)
  Salt, 1/2 t (3 ml)
  Sugar, 2 T (30 ml)
  Red wine vinegar, 2 T (30 ml)
  Chili oil to taste

- Step 2. Cooking oil, 2 T (30 ml)
  Eggs, 2
  Pre-cooked rice, 3 C (720 ml)

- Step 3. Cooked ham*,
    sliced, 6 oz (170 g)
  Scallions, 2
  Frozen green peas,
    1 C (240 ml)
  Bean sprouts, 2 C (480 ml)
  Salt
  Pepper
  Roasted peanuts, 2 T (30 ml),
    optional

INSTRUCTIONS

Wash cucumbers. Without peeling, slice thinly by hand or using a food processor. Mix with additional ingredients listed. Serve chilled or at room temperature.

Heat wok until very hot. While wok heats, beat eggs. Add oil to wok, then add eggs. Stir until eggs become firmly set. Add rice. Stir intermittently to allow some of the rice to get crusty as this will enhance its flavor.

Meanwhile, julienne-cut ham. Dice scallions. Add items to rice (Step 2) in the following order, pausing each time to stir briefly: Peas, ham, bean sprouts, scallions. Season with salt and pepper to taste. Garnish with peanuts.

* Substitute any leftover meat, chicken, seafood or cooked beans. Drain and chop before using.

INGREDIENTS AND EQUIPMENT

PERISHABLES	PANTRY ITEMS	EQUIPMENT
pickling cucumbers 1 1b (450g)	red wine vinegar	wok or large skillet
cooked ham, ready-sliced or any	cooking oil	
leftovers	roasted peanuts (optional)	
frozen green peas	chili oil	
bean sprouts 2cups (480ml)		
eggs		
cooked rice, chilled		
scallions		

PAN-FRIED TOFU

EGGPLANT SALAD

RICE

SERVES 2 TO 3

The American studying Chinese in Taipei said in his best Chinese, "I love to eat tofu!" The whole room burst into laughter. What did he say? What was wrong? The mystified student later found out that in Chinese slang, "eating tofu" means "taking advantage of a younger woman". Perhaps because tofu is tender and fair and cheap!

INGREDIENTS	INSTRUCTIONS
• Step 1. Tofu, firm, 1 lb (450 g) Wood ears, 2 T (30 ml)	Remove tofu from package and set on plate to drain. Soak wood ears in warm water.
• Step 2. Rice, 3/4 C (180 ml) Water, 1 1/2 C (360 ml)	Wash rice. Place with water in rangetop casserole. Bring to boil over high heat. Boil for 1 minute, uncovered. Turn heat to the lowest setting, cover and simmer for 5 to 10 minutes. Leave it covered until dinner time. Don't stir. As it cooks, do the following:
• Step 3. Oriental eggplant, 1 lb (450 g) Ginger, 1 thick slice Sugar, 1 t (5 ml) Garlic powder, 1/2 t (3 ml) Soy sauce, 1 T (15 ml) Rice vinegar, 1 T (15 ml) Sesame oil, 1 t (5 ml) Cilantro or diced scallion	Scrub eggplant and slice into thin pieces. Spread pieces on plate, sprinkle with 1 T (15 ml) of water. Cover and microwave on high for 3 minutes. Stir and repeat. (Or steam until eggplant is cooked). Spread eggplant on a different plate to cool. Use a garlic press to squeeze ginger juice onto the eggplant when slightly cooled. Mix eggplant with remaining ingredients listed, except for the cilantro. Garnish with cilantro. Serve chilled or at room temperature.
• Step 4. Cooking oil, 2 T (30 ml) Salt, 1/2 t (3 ml) Black pepper, 1/4 t (1 ml) Scallion, 1	Slice tofu (Step 1) into pieces 2/3 inch (2 cm) thick. Heat large skillet until very hot. Add oil and swirl to spread evenly. Add tofu and brown one side over high heat while sprinkling half of the salt and pepper over the top. Turn and repeat. Don't worry if some of the tofu breaks apart or becomes slightly burned. While waiting for tofu to brown, dice scallion and drain wood ears (Step 1). Push tofu to one side of pan and add wood ears to other side of pan. Stir wood ears for 1 minute. Then stir everything together and transfer onto serving platter. Garnish with scallion.

INGREDIENTS AND EQUIPMENT

PERISHABLES	PANTRY ITEMS		EQUIPMENT
firm tofu 1 lb (450g)	garlic powder	sesame oil	large skillet
eggplant 1 lb (450g)	soy sauce	wood ears	small rangetop casserole
cilantro (or scallions)	rice vinegar	rice	microwave oven
fresh ginger	cooking oil		
scallion			

MA PO TOFU

BROCCOLI WITH SESAME SEEDS

RICE

SERVES 2 TO 3

So you think tofu means bland? Try this:

	INGREDIENTS	INSTRUCTIONS
• Step 1.	Soft tofu, 1 lb (450 g)	Lift tofu out of water and set on a plate to drain off excess liquid.
• Step 2.	Rice, 3/4 C (180 ml) Water, 1 1/2 C (360 ml)	Rinse rice. Place with water in a samll rangetop casserole. Bring to boil over high heat. Boil uncovered for 1 minute, turn heat to the lowest setting, cover and simmer for 5 to 10 minutes. Keep covered until dinner time. Don't stir. As the rice cooks, do the following:
• Step 3.	Broccoli florets, 1/2 lb (230 g) Sugar, 1/2 t (3 ml) Oyster sauce, 1 t (5 ml) Soy sauce, 2 t (10 ml) Sesame oil, 1 t (5 ml) Water, 1 T (15 ml) White sesame seeds, 2 T (30 ml)	Place broccoli on a plate. Sprinkle with 1 T water. Cover and microware at high for 1 1/2 minutes. Plunge into a pan of cold water to cool. Drain mix the remaning ingredients except sesame seeds. Pour over broccoli and toss. Transfer to a serving platter and garnish with sesame seeds. Serve cold or at room temperature.
• Step 4.	Fermented black beans, 　1 T (15 ml) Garlic, 3 cloves Ginger, 3 slices Hot bean paste, 1 T (15 ml) 　or to taste	Rinse black beans. Mince beans, ginger and garlic together. Combine with the remaining ingredients.
• Step 5.	Cooking oil, 2 T (30 ml) Ground pork, beef or chicken, 　1/4 lb (110 g) Salt, 1/2 t (3 ml) or to taste Sugar, 1 t (5 ml) Soy sauce, 1 T (15 ml) Water, 1/4 C (60 ml)	Heat wok until very hot. Add oil. Stirs briefly items prepared in Step 4. Add meat and stir until color changes. Turn spatula around and cut tofu into pieces. Alternate between cutting and turning. Add salt, sugar and soy sauce, stir. Add water and bring to boil. Turn heat to medium and simmer for 3 minutes. Stir occasinally.
• Step 6.	Scallion, 1 Cornstarch, 1 T (15 ml) Water, 1 T (15 ml) Sichuan pepper powder, a few 　dashes	Meanwhile, chop scallion. Make a paste with cornstarch and water. Dribble the paste into wok and stir at the same time. Stop when sauce is thick enough. Discard remaining paste. Transfer into a serving bowl. Sprinkte Sichuan pepper and scallion.

INGREDIENTS AND EQUIPMENT

PERISHABLES	PANTRY ITEMS		EQUIPMENT
soft tofu 1 lb (450g)	corn starch	oyster sauce	wok or large
ground meat, any kind 1/4 lb (110g)	cooking oil	fermented black beans	skillet
broccoli florets 1/2 lb (230g)	soy sauce	sichuan powder	microwave oven
fresh ginger	hot bean paste	white sesame seeds	
scallions	rice	garlic	
	sesame oil		

Appendix

HANDY BILINGUAL SHOPPING LIST

(make a copy for shopping)

HERBS AND SPICES

chili 辣椒 A24, B21*
cilantro 香菜 A26
ginger 薑 A23
scallion 蔥 A25

MEAT PRODUCTS

Chinese barbecued pork 叉燒 A11
   (*Char siu*)
Chinese sausages 香腸 A12

FRESH WHEAT AND RICE PRODUCTS

Chinese noodles, fresh 新鮮麵 A4, A5
Jiaotze skin 餃子皮 A6
mooshu wrappers 單餅 A8
rice noodles, fresh 沙河粉 A10
   (*sha ho fen*)
scallion rolls 花捲 A1
silver thread rolls 銀絲捲 A3
spring roll wrappers
(Shanghai spring roll wrappers)
   上海春捲皮 A7, A9
steamed buns 饅頭 A2

BEAN PRODUCTS

pressed tofu, brown 豆腐干 A30
pressed tofu, five-fragrant 五香豆腐干 A31
tofu, firm 老豆腐 A28
tofu, soft 嫩豆腐 A29

FRESH VEGETABLES

baby carrots 小胡蘿蔔 A14
bean sprouts 綠豆芽 A21
Chinese chives 韭菜 A19
lotus root 藕 A18
Oriental eggplant 小茄子 A17
pickling cucumbers 小黃瓜 A20
red-in-snow 雪裡紅 A22
Shanghai choy 青江菜 A16
snow peas 雪豆 A27
soy beans 毛豆 A13
watercress 西洋菜 A15

CONDIMENTS

chili oil 辣油
hoisin sauce 海鮮醬
hot bean sauce 辣豆瓣醬
oyster sauce 蠔油
rice vinegar 米醋
rice wine 米酒
sesame oil 麻油
soy sauce, dark 老抽
soy sauce, light 生抽
soy sauce, regular 醬油

CANNED GOODS

baby corn 玉米筍
bamboo shoots 筍 B20
bamboo shoots, braised 紅燜筍尖
golden needle mushrooms 金針菇 B16
pickled leeks 蕎頭 B15
Red-in-Snow 雪裡紅 A22
Sichuan vegetable 榨菜 B13
soy sauce cucumbers 醬瓜 B11
Tianjin vegetable 天津冬菜 B14
water chestnuts 荸薺，馬蹄
wheat gluten 麵筋 B12

DRIED GOODS

bean threads 粉絲
black mushrooms, dried 香菇 B5
chili, dried 乾辣椒 B21
Chinese noodles, dried 乾麵 B6
fermented black beans 豆豉 B8
golden needles 金針 B3, B4
rice sticks 米粉 B7
sesame seeds 芝麻
Sichuan pepper powder 花椒粉
Sichuan peppercorns 花椒 B17
shrimp, dried 蝦米 B22
star anise 八角 B2
tangerine peels, dried 陳皮 B18, B19
wood ears 木耳

CANNED SIDE DISHES

fish paste, fried 魚醬
pork paste 肉醬
shredded fish 魚鬆 B1
vegetarian noodle sauce 素肉醬

DESSERTS

almond cookies 杏仁餅
candied ginger 薑糖
candied kumquat 金桔 B9
egg rolls 蛋捲 B10
loquat (in can) 枇杷
lychee (in can) 荔枝
peanut candy 花生糖
sesame candy 芝麻糖
sesame cookies 芝麻餅

* The numbers identifying the ingredients are keyed to the photograph on P.142.

A FEW HELPFUL HINTS

* Don't fuss over precise timing or measurements. The measurements in this book are guidelines rather than strict requirements. Time and experience will tell you how much soy sauce, sesame oil, etc., to use.
* Have the butcher/meat department slice meat.
* Have the butcher/meat department grind meat in bulk, then wrap it in 1/4 lb. (110 grams) or 1/2 C (120 ml) packages and stick them in the freezer for later use.
* Use canned black mushrooms. Dried mushrooms take 30 minutes in warm water to soften.
* Use ready-cut vegetables from local supermarket salad bar.
* Select pre-sliced/pre-shredded canned variety of water chestnuts, Sichuan vegetables, etc.
* Use microwave oven to blanch vegetables (You avoid boiling a pot of water).
* Use microwave to steam (You avoid having to take out the steamer and to boil water).

* For stir-frying, set wok over high-heat; do some other things while wok heats.
* Marinate meat in the store container. It saves washing another plate.
* Don't make the marinade first and then mix it with meat. Throw everything into the meat and mix. Let the meat stand at room temperature while you do other things.
* Smash the garlic clove with the side of a cleaver or a large knife to loosen skin for easy peeling (see p.44).
* A slice of ginger is the size of a quarter, more or less. Don't peel it. The skin is the most flavorful part.
* Use the same cookware to cook and serve.
* Substitute bread, rolls, flour tortilla, and pita bread for rice, and various Chinese bread and wrappers. You can make any bread taste almost Chinese if you steam it by wrapping in damp kitchen towel and microwaving it briefly. Overheating would make it chewy.

FOOL-PROOF RICE

If your rice comes out looking like mush or is undercooked, you are probably not using the proper ratio of rice to water. The recipe in this book lists the proper ratio, so just follow the directions and you shouldn't have any problem. In general, however, the proper ratio of rice to water is as follows:

1/2 C (120 ml) rice   1 C plus 2 T (270 ml) water
1 C (240 ml) rice   2 C (480 ml) water
2 C (480 ml) rice   3 1/2 C (840 ml) water
4 C (960 ml) rice   5 C (1200 ml) water

If the rice boils over, just keep the cover ajar for the first 2 to 3 minutes of simmering.

Rice Cooker: The rice cooker is easy to use, virtually fool-proof and will keep the rice hot until ready to serve. However, you have to transfer the rice from the cooker to a serving bowl; and you have to wash two items. It is much easier to cook rice in a casserole dish and serve in it.

DOUBLING THE RECIPES

You can double or triple the serving amount of any recipe except when stir-frying. If you double a stir-fried recipe, you double the trouble, you get a dish that looks and tastes steamed--a definite No No. To double the serving amount of a stir-fried recipe, you must first stir-fry one serving and then separately stir-fry the second serving.

EQUIPMENT

You don't need any special equipment to prepare the recipes presented in this cookbook, but there are a few tools which will make cooking an easier and more enjoyable task.

Cleaver: This is the most versatile piece of equipment in a Chinese kitchen. Use the blade to chop, slice and dice. Use the side of the blade to smash garlic (see p.44) before removing the peel. Select an all-purpose carbon steel cleaver. The blunt end of the blade should be at least 1/8 inch (32 mm) thick. Wipe dry after each use to prevent rusting.

Wok: Select a 14 inch (36 cm) wok made of iron or carbon steel. Avoid aluminum and stainless steel woks, as they cannot withstand the intense heat necessary for stir-frying. A wok with two handles is necessary if you are unable to pick it up one-handed. If you have an electric stove, select a wok with a flat bottom. Season your new wok as follows: First, scrub the interiorwith scouring powder, a steel pad and hot water to remove the protective coating applied by the manufacturer. Rinse and dry with paper towels. Next, rub vegetable oil all around the interior of the wok. From now on, only wash the wok with a nylon brush and hot water. Don't use any detergent. Eventually the wok's interior will develop a black coating. This is the sign of a well-seasoned wok. In addition to the wok, you may want to purchase a **dome-shaped cover** which will convert the wok into a steamer or smoker. You will also find it handy to use a carbon steel or stainless steel **spatula** which fits the contours of the wok.

Microwave Oven: Some recipes in this book were prepared with the assistance of a 650-watt microwave oven.

Steamer: If you don't own a microwave, you will need a steamer to heat Chinese breads. In general, when preparing the recipes in this book, put the item to be steamed on a plate and place the plate in the steamer. Cover and steam until the item is ready.

Make-shift Steamer: If you don't have a steamer, you can create one in the following manner:

Place an empty can, with both ends removed, in a large pot. Add water until it is 1 inch (3 cm) below the top of the can. Set food to be steamed on a heat-proof dish and place the dish on top of the can.

Cover the pot. Bring water to a boil. Keep the water at a boil until the food is ready. Frequently check the level of the water and add more boiling water if necessary.

Food Processor: A food processor saves time when it comes to slicing and julienne-cutting vegetables.

Skillet: Select a large, heavy skillet with a cover, preferably one made of cast iron. Otherwise, use a non-stick skillet.

Sauce Pans: Sauce pans of different sizes will come in handy for boiling noodles and preparing soups.

Casserole Dishes: An ideal casserole dish is one which can be used for cooking on a stove, cooking in a microwave oven, and serving food at the table.

Bowls: If you will be using a microwave oven, select microwave-safe bowls that can also be used to serve food at the table.

Garlic Press: Handy for squeezing juice from ginger.

ADDITIONAL EQUIPMENT

Wooden Chopping Board

Colander

Tongs

Paring Knives

Small Knife with Serrated Edge

Kitchen Shears

Measuring Cups and Spoons

GLOSSARY OF INGREDIENTS

PERISHABLE ITEMS
(Refrigerate)

A14* BABY CARROTS

Miniature carrots, fresh or frozen, usually sold in 1 lb (450 g) packages.

BEAN CURD, see TOFU

A21* BEAN SPROUTS 豆芽

There are two varieties-green and yellow. The recipes in this book use only the green variety. Green bean sprouts have white stems and light green hoods. They can be kept for 2 to 3 days immersed in cold water in the refrigerator.

A24* CHILI PEPPERS 新鮮辣椒

These spicy red or green peppers can be purchased at most supermarkets or at specialty stores. They can be kept in the refrigerator for a couple of weeks.

A11* CHINESE BARBECUED PORK** 叉燒

(Char Siu) This item can be purchased from Chinese restaurants or Chinese grocery stores. It can be eaten alone or stir-fried along with other items. It keeps in the refrigerator for about a week, but Char Siu made that day is the best.

A19* CHINESE CHIVES** 韭菜

This is an Asian vegetable that resembles grass that has not been mowed for a long time.

A4,A5* CHINESE NOODLES, fresh** 新鮮麵

There are two varieties of wheat noodles-those made with eggs (light yellow) and those made without eggs (ivory). Depending on your personal preference you can select thick or thin noodles. They boil very fast, often before the water comes to a second boil. Fresh noodles keep for 2 weeks in refrigerator and 3 months in freezer. If unavailable, use fresh pasta.

A12* CHINESE SAUSAGES** 香腸

Link sausages made of pork or liver. Steam or cook along with other items before eating. They keep for months if refrigerated.

A26* CILANTRO** 香菜

(Chinese Parsley, Fresh Coriander) You love or hate this flat-leaved herb! Sometimes you can even find it in supermarkets. Can be kept in a closed jar in the refrigerator for 2 weeks.

CRAB MEAT, cooked

Cooked crab meat is available in 12 or 16 oz cans at the seafood counter of your local supermarket. The price ranges from high to higher. Your choice depends on your purse and your palate. The crab meat in the cans at the fish counter is much tastier than that in the cans on the shelves, but you can use the latter in stir-fried rice. Crab meat keeps for 2 days in the refrigerator, and 2 months in freezer once the can is opened.

---

* The numbers identifying the ingredients are keyed to the photograph on P.142.

** Available only at Chinese grocery stores or specialty markets.

EGGPLANT

Oriental eggplant A17* are available at Asian grocery stores. They don't need to be peeled. The large, fat kind are found in supermarkets. They must be peeled before slicing. The two are interchangeable, although the latter takes longer to cook.

FISH

The freshness of the fish is more important than its variety. Avoid fish with a strong smell. Select a fish with bulging eyes and shiny scales. If cooking a whole fish, choose one that will fit your microwave or skillet. If you plan to stir-fry, buy a fish with firm meat so that it won't crumble in the wok.

FLOWER ROLLS, see SCALLION ROLLS

A23* GINGER 薑，老薑

Knobby, aromatic root used as a spice. Select ginger with a smooth skin. Ginger will keep for about 2 weeks at room temperature or indefinitely in the refrigerator immersed in any kind of wine in a closed jar. When cooking with ginger, don't bother to peel it. Also, don't be too concerned with the exact size of the slices. When the recipe calls for "a slice of ginger," use a piece approximately the size of a quarter a slight variations in the size hardly affect the taste. Don't use dried ginger or ginger powder as a substitute for fresh ginger.

Occasionally you also find tender *young ginger* in stores. It is usually used as garnish for fish or relish for *dim sum*.

A6* GYOZA SKIN, see JIAOTZE SKINS✦✦ 餃子皮

These round skins, made of flour and water and measuring about 4 inches (10 cm) in diameter are used for wrapping dumpling filling. They can be located in the refrigerator or freezer section of Asian grocery stores, or in the vegetable department of regular supermarkets. They keep for 2 weeks in the refrigerator or 3 months in the freezer. When thawing, wrap in a damp cloth.

A18* LOTUS ROOT✦✦ 藕

A light brown root shaped like salami linked together. When cut into slices, its cross-section looks like a cartwheel. Lotus root can be stewed, stir-fried or made into a salad.

A8* MOOSHU WRAPPERS✦✦ 單餅

(Mandarin Pancakes, Thin Cakes). These round, thin disks made of wheat flour are kept in the refrigerator or freezer sections of Chinese grocery stores. Use for wrapping up Peking duck, mooshu pork or any dish made of cut-up pieces. Wrap in a damp towel when thawing or heating in microwave. They keep for two weeks in refrigerator or 3 months in freezer. You can substitute them with flour tortillas or pita bread.

A17* ORIENTAL EGGPLANT, see EGGPLANT

A20* PICKLING CUCUMBERS 小黃瓜

(Gherkins). Slender, crisp cucumbers, used

---

* The numbers identifying the ingredients are keyed to the photograph on P.142.

✦✦ *Available only at Chinese grocery stores or specialty markets.*

for pickling, stir-frying or cold-mixing. Select firm and bumpy ones.

PRESSED TOFU, see TOFU

A22* RED-IN-SNOW✦✦ 雪裡紅

It is neither red nor white as snow. It is a preserved green vegetable called *yutsai*, the top of whose red roots appears in the early spring when the snow is still on the ground. Available in the United States in barrels (whole) or in cans (chopped). Can be kept for weeks in a jar in the refrigerator.

A10* RICE NOODLES, fresh✦✦ 沙河粉

(*Sha Ho Fen*). Pre-cooked noodles made of rice powder and water. They are packaged in plastic bags and kept in the refrigerator section of Chinese grocery stores. Stir-fry them just as you would cooked noodles. They can be kept in the refrigerator for 1 week.

A1* SCALLION ROLLS✦✦ 花捲

(*Flower Rolls*). Buns made of scallions, vegetable oil and pepper rolled into yeast dough. They are available in the refrigerator section at Chinese grocery stores. When heating rolls in a microwave oven, first wrap them in a damp towel. Can be kept in the refrigerator for 2 weeks or in the freezer for 3 months. If unavailable, use Brown N' Serve sourdough dinner rolls as a substitute.

A25* SCALLIONS 蔥

(Green Onions). Can be kept in a plastic bag in the refrigerator for about 1 week.

A16* SHANGHAI CHOY✦✦ 青江菜

(Baby Bok Choy) A small vegetable with green leaves and a light green stems. If unavailable, use regular bok choy as a substitute, but be sure to remove the bok choy's outer leaves before using.

A3* SILVER THREAD ROLLS✦✦ 銀絲捲

Rolls made of yeast dough, sugar and oil. They are available in the refrigerator or freezer section of Chinese grocery stores. Fresh rolls keep for 2 weeks in the refrigerator or 3 months in the freezer. If heating in a microwave oven, first wrap the rolls in a damp towel. Avoid over-heating as this makes the rolls hard. If unavailable, substitute with Brown N' Serve sourdough dinner rolls.

A27* SNOW PEAS 雪豆

Flat, crescent-shaped pods with tiny peas inside. Snow peas are deliciously crunchy and colorful. To prepare, nip off ends and pull off strings. They keep in a plastic bag in the refrigerator for 1 week. Frozen snow peas are not a good substitute because they lack crunchiness.

A13* SOY BEANS✦✦ 毛豆

Soy beans resemble baby lima beans. In fact, baby lima beans can be used as a substitute if soy beans are unavailable. They come packaged frozen in plastic bags.

A7,A9* SPRING ROLL WRAPPERS✦✦ 春捲皮

These thin wrappers come in two varieties-

---

* The numbers identifying the ingredients are keyed to the photograph on P.142.

✦✦ *Available only at Chinese grocery stores or specialty markets.*

round or square. They are packaged 25 or 50 apiece in plastic packages which are stored in the refrigerator section of Asian grocery stores. You can eat them straight out of the package or you can first wrap them in a damp towel and heat them for 1 minute in the microwave. Of course you can also use them to make spring rolls. Fresh wrappers can be kept for 2 weeks in the refrigerator or 3 months in the freezer. Use flour tortillas or pita bread as a substitute bread. Don't confuse them with the thick, doughy egg roll wrappers. They are raw.

A2* STEAMED BUNS♦♦ 饅頭

(*Mantow*). Buns made from yeast dough, found in refrigerator or freezer section of Chinese grocery stores. They are bland-tasting, but they complement flavorful dishes. Before eating, reheat by steaming, or wrap in a damp kitchen towel and heat in the microwave. Don't microwave overlong or the buns will turn chewy. Fresh buns keep for 2 weeks in the refrigerator or 3 months in the freezer. If unavailable, substitute with Brown N' Serve sourdough dinner rolls.

TOFU 豆腐

(Bean Curd, *Doufu*) Tofu is bean curd processed from soy bean milk. It is inexpensive, and very high in protein. It is also low in saturated fat. Fresh, plain tofu is ivory-colored and has the consistency of custard. It comes in three varieties: soft A29, firm or extra firm A28. It is available in separate square pieces in Asian grocery stores and in vacuum—sealed packages at supermarkets. The former should be immersed in chilled water and kept in the refrigerator for 5 days, change water every day. Some recipes in this book call for pressed tofu. Pressed Tofu 豆腐干 A30*, available in Chinese grocery stores, comes in various sizes and in colors ranging from ivory to dark brown. Use the large, light brown variety when preparing these recipes. Another form of pressed tofu, called Five-fragrant Pressed Tofu 五香豆腐干 A31* , is also available in Chinese grocery stores. It is seasoned with soy sauce, sugar and spices. You can eat it as a tasty side dish or snack. Do not freeze any of the above varieties of tofu.

A15* WATERCRESS 西洋芹

A delicate green plant with soft stems and small leaves. Americans use it in salad and the Chinese use it in soups or to line platters for steamed meatballs.

---

* The numbers identifying the ingredients are keyed to the photograph on P.142.

♦♦ *Available only at Chinese grocery stores or specialty markets.*

PANTRY ITEMS
(Refrigerate after opening)

Underlined items are an essential part of your pantry.

ALMONDS, roasted

Use as a garnish, slivered or whole.

A32* BABY CORN 玉米筍

(Young Corn) Miniature cobs of corn available in cans. Use in salads or for stir-fried dishes. After opening can, immerse unused portions in a jar filled with water and keep in the refrigerator for 2 weeks, changing the water twice a week.

B20* BAMBOO SHOOTS 筍

Canned bamboo shoots are often available in regular supermarkets. Buy ready-sliced ones to save time. After opening can, keep unused portions immersed in water in refrigerator up to 2 weeks. Change the water twice a week.

BAMBOO SHOOTS, BRAISED WITH CHILI♦♦ 辣椒油燜筍尖

Bamboo shoots braised in hot spices, available in cans or jars. Use as a side dish. Keep unused portion enclosed in jar in the refrigerator for up to 3 months.

BEAN THREADS♦♦ 粉絲

(Cellophane Noodles, Peastarch Noodles). These high-protein noodles are made from mung beans. They look almost like rice sticks but packaged in small bundles in plastic bags.

BLACK MUSHROOMS 香菇

Dried mushroom B5* are the best kind, but they must be soaked in warm water for 30 minutes before use. Acceptable substitutes are canned black mushrooms, sold in some Chinese grocery stores under the label Po Ku Mushrooms.

CANDIED GINGER♦♦ 薑糖

Use as a dessert.

B9* CANDIED KUMQUAT♦♦ 金桔

Use as a dessert.

CHILI OIL 辣油

(Hot Oil, Hot Pepper Oil) Made from sesame oil and chili. Available at Asian grocery stores and at some regular supermarkets. Keep in pantry for 3 months or in refrigerator indefinitely.

B21* CHILIES, dried 乾辣椒

The smaller chilies are hotter than the larger ones, so make your choice accordingly. Keep indefinitely in the pantry.

B6* CHINESE NOODLES, dried♦♦ 乾麵

These dried noodles are made of wheat flour, comes in different thicknesses. The very thin noodles take only 1 to 2 minutes to cook in boiling water. If you are unable to find Chinese noodles, use thinnest spaghetti you can find, which takes at least 5 minutes to cook.

CHINESE VINEGAR, see RICE VINEGAR

---

* The numbers identifying the ingredients are keyed to the photograph on P.142.

♦♦ Available only at Chinese grocery stores or specialty markets.

CHINESE WINE, see RICE WINE

COOKING OIL

Any vegetable oil labeled salad oil, peanut oil, soy oil, sunflower oil, granola oil, safflower oil or pure olive oil is suitable for cooking Chinese food. Virgin olive oil is too strong-tasting and sesame oil tends to produce smoke, so neither is best for stir-frying.

CORNSTARCH

Used for thickening sauces and soups, also in marinade to make meat tender.

DACE, fried**

Dace is a fish which had been fried and seasoned. It comes packaged in an oval can, either with or without black beans. It can serve as a side dish, although it is high in sodium and fat.

DARK SOY SAUCE, see SOY SAUCE

DRIED MUSHROOMS, see BLACK MUSHROOMS

DRIED TANGERINE PEEL, see TANGERINE PEEL

DRIED TIGER LILIES, see GOLDEN NEEDLES

B10* EGG ROLLS** 蛋捲

When the Chinese speak of egg rolls they are referring to cookies made of flour, sugar, eggs, vanilla and shortening, not the "rabbit food" wrapped in doughy skin and deep-fried. They come in cans. Serve them with sherbet or ice cream as a dessert.

B8* FERMENTED BLACK BEANS** 豆豉

(Black Beans) Black beans which have been fermented and preserved in ginger and salt. They are packaged in plastic bags or cylindrical paper boxes. Although pungent, they add a delightful flavor to food. Keep them in the pantry indefinitely. Don't worry if a white powder appears on the surface of the beans—it is only salt. Rinse the beans before using.

FISH PASTE, fried** 魚醬

Spicy minced fish fried in oil. Packaged in small cans. Use as a side dish.

GARLIC

Use fresh garlic if possible. Otherwise use ready-chopped garlic packed in oil in jars, garlic powder or dried garlic flakes. Don't add powder or flakes directly to the hot oil as they would burn. Instead, add them to your marinade.

B16* GOLDEN NEEDLE MUSHROOMS** 金針菇

These mushrooms resemble bean sprouts. They are usually sold in cans. Keep leftover portions immersed in water in a closed jar in your refrigerator for up to 2 weeks. Change the water twice a week.

B3,B4* GOLDEN NEEDLES** 金針

(Tiger Lily Buds, Dried Tiger Lilies). There are golden and brown varieties. Soak in water for 10 minutes before using. They keep in the pantry for months.

The numbers identifying the ingredients are keyed to the photograph on P.142.

**Available only at Chinese grocery stores or specialty markets.*

HOISIN SAUCE 海鮮醬

Sweet-tasting sauce made from soy beans, sugar, salt, flour, garlic and chili. It is used for marinating, seasoning, or as a condiment. It comes in cans or in jars. To keep indefinitely, transfer canned hoisin sauce into a jar, close it and place it in the refrigerator. High in sodium. Use Sweet Bean Sauce as a substitute, which is also salty.

HOT BEAN PASTE♦♦ 辣豆瓣醬

(Sichuan Hot Bean Paste, Chili Paste). Made of fermented beans, salt and chili. It comes packaged in jars or in cans, but the jarred variety is far superior. It keeps for 3 months at room temperature or indefinitely in the refrigerator. If you are on a low sodium diet, use sparingly or use chili oil instead.

HOT OIL, see CHILI OIL

JAHTSAI, see SICHUAN VEGETABLE

LOQUAT♦♦ 枇杷

(*Pi-pa*) A small, orange-yellow fruit which is usually packaged in syrup in cans. Use as a dessert.

LYCHEE♦♦ 荔枝

(*Lichee*) A fruit with a rough red skin, white translucent pulp and brown pit. Occasionally it is available fresh, but more often it is packaged in cans in syrup. Use as a dessert.

MANDARIN ORANGES

Use as a dessert alone or combined with cookies.

MANGOES, dried

Use as a dessert.

MOCK MEAT, see WHEAT GLUTEN

ONIONS

Use whichever variety you like best.

ORIENTAL SESAME SEED OIL, see SESAME OIL

OYSTER SAUCE 蠔油

Thick brown sauce made from oyster extract, salt, soy sauce and spices. Sometimes m.s.g. is added. Keeps for months at room temperature and indefinitely in the refrigerator. If you are on a low-sodium diet, use a samll quantity.

PEANUT CANDY

The Chinese have their own version. It makes a delicious dessert for Chinese meals.

PEPPER, ground

Use white pepper if preparing a mild-tasting dish or seafood. Use black pepper when preparing a robust dish.

B15* PICKLED LEEKS♦♦ 蕎頭

The bulb of a plant of the garlic family, pickled in vinegar and salt. Use as a side dish or a spice. Can be kept in a jar in the refrigerator indefinitely.

---

* The numbers identifying the ingredients are keyed to the photograph on P.142.

♦♦ Available only at Chinese grocery stores or specialty markets.

PINEAPPLE CHUNKS, canned

Use as a dessert.

PORK PASTE, fried✦✦ 肉醬

Fried minced pork, packaged in small cans. Tastes salty and spicy. Can be used as a side dish or as a sauce over boiled noodles.

RED WINE VINEGAR, see RICE VINEGAR

RICE

The staple of the Asian diet. Long-grain rice is fluffier and less sticky than short-grain rice. Both are available in regular supermarkets. Glutinous rice or sweet rice is a special variety only available in Asian grocery stores, it is used in sweets.

B7* RICE STICKS✦✦ 米粉

Long, brittle noodles, made of rice flour. They don't need to be boiled; just soak them in warm water and stir-fry. Rice sticks look almost like bean threads.

RICE VINEGAR✦✦ 米醋

(Chinese Vinegar) A mild vinegar made from rice wine. Most recipes in this book call for white rice vinegar, which is as clear as water. Wine vinegar can be used as a substitute, but use only half the amount you would of rice vinegar. Red wine vinegar is often used in sweet and sour dishes to create a tangy taste.

RICE WINE✦✦ 米酒

A mild cooking wine made from rice, low in alcohol content. In Chinese cooking, wine is used to make meat tender, to subdue unpleasant odors of poultry and seafood, and to add zest to vegetables. Only a very small amount is used. If rice wine is unavailable, almost any type of wine will do.

SALT

Use table salt.

SESAME CANDY✦✦

There are black and white varieties, use as a dessert.

SESAME COOKIES✦✦

Made of sesame seeds, flour, sugar, vanilla and shortening.

SESAME OIL 麻油

(Sesame Seed Oil, Oriental Sesame Oil) Extract of roasted sesame seeds, dark brown in color and aromatic. When stir-frying, pour in cooking oil first, then sesame oil. Sesame oil has a low smoking point, so pouring it directly into a hot wok will create smoke clouds. Buy a small quantity each time. It keeps in the pantry for 3 months or indefinitely in the refrigerator. Shake refrigerated oil before using. *Do not use* the odorless sesame oil, made from raw seeds, sold at health food stores as a substitute.

SESAME PASTE✦✦ 芝麻醬

(Sesame Seed Paste) This is a paste made of ground roasted sesame seeds. Its consistency is similar to that of peanut butter, but it is darker in color. Mix it slowly with water or broth to create a smooth paste before using with salads or

---

* The numbers identifying the ingredients are keyed to the photograph on P.142.

✦✦ Available only at Chinese grocery stores or specialty markets.

as a condiment. It keeps in the pantry for 3 months or indefinitely in the refrigerator. If unavailable you can substitute it with smooth peanut butter mixed with some sesame oil. But do not use *Tahini*, a paste made of raw sesame seeds, as a substitute.

SESAME SEEDS

There are two kinds-black and white. Use them as a garnish, either raw or roasted. To roast: bake at 200 °F (95 °C) for 10 minutes. Keeps for 3 months in the pantry in a closed jar or indefinitely in the refrigerator.

B1* SHREDDED FISH✦✦ 魚鬆

Fluffy, seasoned fish shreds, sold in jars or reclosable cans. Use as a side dish.

B22* SHRIMP, dried✦✦ 蝦米

Pungent and salty. Packaged in plastic bags. Keep indefinitely in the pantry in a closed jar, away from your gourmet cats. Fresh shrimp cannot be used as a substitute.

SICHUAN HOT BEAN PASTE, see HOT BEAN PASTE

SICHUAN PEPPER, ground✦✦ 花椒粉

Available at Chinese food stores in bottles. Or, you can purchase Sichuan peppercorns and grind them in a pepper mill yourself (they will be much more aromatic).

B17* SICHUAN PEPPERCORNS✦✦ 花椒

(Flower Peppers, Anise Peppers) Reddish-brown peppercorns with husks. They taste milder than regular black pepper, but are very aromatic and produce a numbing sensation. They are sold in plastic bags. Transfer into an airtight jar and store in the pantry.

B13* SICHUAN VEGETABLE✦✦ 榨菜

(Sichuan Preserved Vegetable, *Jahtsai*) Made from an olive-colored vegetable from Sichuan province, preserved in red chili and salt. Used as a spice or condiment. Sold by the pound or in cans. Buy the shredded variety. Once you open the can, transfer the contents into a jar and keep in the refrigerator. Rinse with cold water before using unless you want it to be very salty and spicy.

SOY SAUCE

Made from fermented soy beans, wheat, yeast and salt. There are many varieties available. Thin Soy Sauce 生抽, is used when cooking chicken, seafood or other foods. It is lighter in appearance and milder in taste than Dark Soy Sauce 老抽, which is used for stewing or when you want a robust tasting dish. When no particular kind is specified, use thin soy sauce. Low sodium soy sauce is now available for those who are reducing salt intake.

B11* SOY SAUCE CUCUMBERS✦✦ 醬瓜，切條黃瓜

(Pickled Cucumbers) Cucumbers preserved in soy sauce and sugar. They are sold in cans or in jars. They can be kept in the refrigerator in a jar for months. Use as a seasoning or a side dish.

The numbers identifying the ingredients are keyed to the photograph on P.142.

✦✦ *Available only at Chinese grocery stores or specialty markets.*

B2* **STAR ANISE**✦✦ 八角

Star-shaped, aromatic spice. It smells like licorice. Use it sparingly. It is sold in plastic bags. After opening the bag, transfer its contents to an airtight jar. It will keep indefinitely at room temperature.

SUGAR

Use either refined or raw sugar.

B19* **TANGERINE PEELS, dried**✦✦ 陳皮

The dried skin of a tangerine. Soaked in hot water and minced and used as a spice. Don't confuse it with the smaller peels (**B18***) which can be used as a snack. Keep indefinitely in the pantry in a closed jar.

B14* **TIANJIN PRESERVED VEGETABLE**✦✦ 天津冬菜

(Tianjin Vegetable) Chinese cabbage preserved with salt, garlic and spices. Packaged in a ceramic jar. It is used in stewed and stir-fried dishes. It will keep indefinitely at room temperature if its ceramic jar is tightly sealed.

TIGER LILY BUDS, see GOLDEN NEEDLES

TREE EARS, see WOOD EARS

VEGETARIAN NOODLE SAUCE✦✦ 素肉醬

Use this sauce as a garnish for noodles.

VEGETABLE STEAK, see WHEAT GLUTEN

VINEGAR, see RICE VINEGAR

WALNUTS

Use as a garnish.

WATER CHESTNUTS 荸薺，馬蹄

Bulbs of an aquatic plant. They are crunchy and slightly sweet. Don't chop them too fine which would destroy the crunchy texture. Put any unused portion immersed in water in a closed jar in the refrigerator for up to 2 weeks. Change the water twice a week. Fresh water chestnuts at Asian grocery stores are superior in flavor and texture, but they must be peeled before use.

B12* **WHEAT GLUTEN**✦✦ 麵筋

(Vegetable Steak, Mock Meat) The protein extracted from whole wheat dough, puffed up in hot oil and cooked to resemble meat dishes. Sold in jars or cans, it can become Mock Abalone 素鮑魚 , Mock Duck 素鴨 , Mock Curried Chicken 咖哩素雞肉 , etc. or remain just plain Wheat Gluten. Use as a side dish as is, or Stir-fry in place of meat.

B23 ***WOOD EARS**✦✦ 木耳 **(Tree Ears)**

Dark, thin mushrooms which grow on wood. Dried wood ears are available in Chinese grocery stores. They must be soaked in warm water for 5 minutes before use. Buy the small variety, known as Sichuan wood ears, if possible. Keep indefinitely in a closed jar or bag in the pantry.

---

* *The numbers identifying the ingredients are keyed to the photograph on P.142.*

✦✦ *Available only at Chinese grocery stores or specialty markets.*

INDEX

There are several advantages to Cooking by Methods. Frist, Once you learn the method of Stir-Frying, you can stir-fry beef, pork, fish and other food groups in essentially the some way. Second, you can plan menus to accent contrasts in taste, color and texture. Third, you can plan your time wisely and prepare elaborate meals in flash.

YOU CAN COOK ANYTHING CHINESE!

by Yee Yo

A completely NEW approach to cooking Chinese food!
This easy-to-follow guide learn the eleven-most popular methods of preparing Chinese cuisine including stir-frying, steaming and roasting. Additionally, cleaver cutting method such as slicing and shredding, helpful hints, handy shopping list and menu planning are included.

With this book in hand, you'll be able to mix and match ingredients and cooking methods to produce the Chinese meal of you culinary dreams!

210 x 285mm/ 8 ¹/4 x 11 ¹/4 inches, paperback, 167 pp, over 300 color plates
Suggested retail price: US$ 14.95
ISBN 0-914929-82-8